22/8/20

WINKS AND WAGGING TAILS

Reminiscences of a
Nineteen-Forties London vet

BY ROBERT E. ABLETT

COPYRIGHT

Copyright 2011 Robert E. Ablett

First published in 2011

The right of Robert E Ablett to be identified as the author of this work has been asserted by him in accordance with the Copyright, Design and Patents Act 1988.

All rights reserved. No part of this publication may be reproduced, stored in a retrieval system, or transmitted, in any form or by any means, electronic, mechanical, photocopying, recording or otherwise, without the prior permission of the author.

This book is sold subject to the condition that it shall not, by ways of trade or otherwise, be lent, re-sold, hired out, or otherwise circulated without the prior consent of the author in any form of binding or cover other than that in which it is published and without a similar condition being imposed on the subsequent purchaser.

Published by Telba Press
1 The Pitchens
Wroughton
Wilts SN4 0RU

Email: telba@mac.com

ISBN 978-0-9555098-1-0

ACKNOWLEDGEMENTS

This book is dedicated to all those people, from The Royal family to the costermongers, who 'stuck it out' in London during the war years and who were able to belie the image that London was a city of gloom, fear and despondency.

DEDICATION

My thanks are to all who have heard these reminiscences on many occasions but still urged me to put them into print. Special thanks to Anne, Paul, Judith and Ursula.

Special thanks also to Sue Killoran for her technical help, to Amber for her illustrations and to Ben Hayward for all his help with the typesetting and book design.

CHILDHOOD DREAMS

The Prologue

CHAPTER I

GRADUATION

Graduation Day at the Royal Veterinary College in 1947 was not a very elaborate or frilly affair – no caps or gowns. We sat in rows in a temporary room, set aside for special occasions, in the main building in Streatley. We wore clean shirts, which were mainly ex-airforce blue – clothes rationing, food rationing and fuel rationing were very rigorously enforced – and we led a very Spartan life. No-one could afford a new suit. As usual, with the name beginning 'Ab', I was the first to be called up to the desk, which was set out in front of the rows of chairs. There were only about 30 students graduating. I walked forward, signed the oath, shook hands with the visiting dignitary from the Royal College of Veterinary surgeons, received my diploma and went back to my chair.

That was it, I was now a Member of the Royal College of Veterinary Surgeons and my boyhood ambition had been achieved.

There were few relatives to clap – only those who lived nearby were able to make the journey at such short notice.

We had to say "goodbye" to Streatley but we had been lucky to have been moved to such a picturesque Berkshire village. Streatley was a really wonderful place to spend two years' learning one's profession.

There was little time and less money to celebrate. The last part of the final exams had ended two days previously, and the results had been pinned to the notice-board only on the previous day.

After the formalities were over, there was the cycle ride back to my digs in Wallingford, bags to be packed ready for the journey home the next day. There was a little sadness, as one of the group of four of us, who had stuck together over the four years' training, had 'pipped' one part of the finals and had to retake it the next Christmas. The three of us said our 'goodbyes'. One of them, David Barnett, with whom I had shared 'digs' for two years, joined the Ministry of Agriculture and we never met again. The other I subsequently saw by chance in London, and he was heading for Canada with his Dutch wife.

The next day, I cycled to Goring station with a suitcase and a microscope, got out at Paddington, cycled along Praed

Street and the Marylebone Road to St Pancras and travelled to Nottingham and home. All my books had been sent off by rail a few days earlier.

There was no time to celebrate at home in Bulwell, near Nottingham, as my mother, sister and I were to go on holiday the next day for a six-day trip to Boscastle.

Two days at home again and then to London and work.

CHILDHOOD DREAMS

We always had animals. All of my life, animals have been, in one form or another, members of the family. Dogs, cats, white mice, guinea pigs, chicken, lizards and stick insects established themselves into the family clan.

It was as a 'sop' for my going to school for the first time, that my sister and I were each given a puppy in the July before starting school in September. The two young smooth fox terrier pups were immediately named 'Sausage' and 'Mash' but they survived only for three or four weeks. It would seem that they were purchased from a pet shop and were obviously incubating distemper when my father bought them. Soon both of them were coughing and sneezing with purulent eyes and nasal discharges. These symptoms progressed to diarrhoea and fits. Attempts were made to establish a cure by dosing them regularly with Benbows dog mixture, an evil smelling concoction, which had little effect on the puppies except to make them vomit more frequently. That, together with the smell from the diarrhoea, made the house unfit to live in. My mother kept the puppies in the kitchen with newspaper all over the floor and she tried to disguise the smell by sprinkling Eau-de-Cologne pretty well everywhere and, to this day, 75 years later, the smell of Eau-de-Cologne makes me feel quite ill.

In the end, the puppies were put down and no more dogs were allowed in the house until the distemper virus had died off.

The following Christmas we were again given another two smooth fox terrier puppies as Christmas presents, which were duly named 'Smash' and 'Grab'. As before, one was a bitch and the other a dog, and I think that my father had an undeclared interest in them, hoping they might mate and produce a litter, which he could sell – he was always in for a 'fast buck'.

These puppies survived for three or four years through their own volition: vaccination against distemper was not an option at the time, but in due course, they also succumbed to distemper. No doubt their survival was due to the fact that we lived in a country village and there was little contact with other dogs.

It was because of the pups that I became good friends with a boy of my age, who lived 'over the road'. My sister was three years older than me and was interested in things other than taking puppies for walks. The boy 'over the road' was just 'Robinson' – Christian names were rarely used but nicknames became common if these nicknames had some real relevance to the boy in question. Robinson joined me in taking the dogs for walks and we both decided that, when we grew up, we would become vets. From that first sad experience, where I had seen the result of disease on the puppies and had to get over the disappointment of seeing them both being taken away to be killed, my dream was to become a qualified vet and tend sick animals. Many children have a dream but, like most dreams, they become unreal and fade as new interests arise, but mine persisted and, thankfully, was fulfilled.

Robinson's father had a sawmill not far away. The Robinsons were a nice family who had the burden of looking after and supporting Mr. Robinson's brother who had suffered from shell-shock in the first world war and was unable to control his limbs or his speech and had shown no improvement over the eleven or twelve years since the end of the war. It was because of Robinson's uncle that his parents thought it best not to have a pet in the house, as they were burdened with his welfare. Smash and Grab then became the 'wards' of the two of us, an arrangement that satisfied everyone in both families.

For a time, I think, Robinson still held on to the dream of qualifying as a vet, but it was never fulfilled. Young Robinson became even more of a friend, as we finished up in the same class at the infants' school.

I was to attend Ashby Infants' school and was filled with trepidation, which turned to outright fear the nearer the first day approached. Ashby was a small village on the outskirts of Scunthorpe. The sense of forthcoming doom was stoked by my mother's perpetual warning that I must have nothing to do with the local ruffians, because they were coarse and not nice to mix with. Not only that, but they used bad language. Not the type of boys you would find in Woking, where my mother and father came from.

As our family assumed themselves to be a cut above the locals, we had to maintain our status, and the best way to confirm this was to dress as Southerners would dress; I was to go to school in shoes and not in boots like all the other boys. Anonymity was immediately destroyed on the first day and I became the target of Carpenter, the school bully who, with his gang, tied me to the only tree in the playground and left me there after the break. The playground was a dry expanse of undulating tarmac with sufficient potholes to cause daily falls and gashed knees, [as I was tall and skinny it became a habit to fall over and find myself going to school with both knees bandaged]. Being tied to a tree on the first day of school was not my idea of fun and established the clear fact that I did not like school, a dislike which remained with me until I finally left school twelve years later. I held back the tears until the teacher, having untied me, asked who had done this to me. Weeping profusely, I told her it was Carpenter and his gang. I had not learnt that it was antisocial to sneak on one's tormentors on the first day of school.

Scunthorpe was not a steel town like Sheffield, where high-quality steel products were manufactured by craftsmen. It was an iron town, which turned out a continuous snake of iron ingots 'pigs' as they were called. Appleby Frodingham Iron Works dominated the whole area with noise, billowing smoke and glowing ore waste. The railway trucks tipped sideways and poured out a flow of waste from the furnaces in the form of molten rock which was to solidify as a porous dark grey slag similar to Aero chocolate but with razor sharp edges. At night the molten slag lit up the sky and the satanic effect was emphasized on cloudy nights when the glow was reflected back to the surrounding countryside.

The town had relaxed with smug satisfaction that the recession was over, the 1930s had arrived and men were back at work knowing that the red sky meant they were producing something worthwhile. The smugness was hinted at in the town's motto 'The Heavens Reflect Our Labour'.

Ten years later, the heavens reflected this labour to German bombers. During the war, everybody prayed for cloudy nights when the glow only penetrated the clouds in a diffuse amorphous hue; this left the Luftwaffe crews knowing they were close, but not knowing when to open the bomb doors. Fortunately, Scunthorpe was rarely bombed, although the air-raid sirens went off very frequently, generally around midnight. In fact, the sirens sounded on the very first night that war was declared but it was merely a false alarm.

Scunthorpe was a tough town to bring up two children, particularly for a woman, born in Woking to an upper working class family, who had high aspirations to move upwards to lower middle class. From the day the young married couple moved to Scunthorpe, the pressure, particularly from my mother, was to get out and move south again. That pressure persisted for another fourteen years. Ambition can be an exhilarating experience, when it is positive, but eroding and consuming when it is unobtainable and my mother's ambition, ingrained in her every action, was not to stay in Scunthorpe for a minute longer than necessary.

This ambition to move down south, was thwarted by my father's initial move after he was 'demobbed'. He became manager of a house-building project at Crosby on the outskirts of Scunthorpe. Many years later, he started his own successful business there and the prospect of moving south diminished as each day passed and as the business developed.

The move from Crosby to Ashby was to mollify my

mother to make up for the continuing necessity to stay near Scunthorpe and my father's business. Little did she know that, before she achieved the final break from Lincolnshire, she would be living back in Scunthorpe again.

Children are resilient, and, although I hated school, Scunthorpe was my home and I found it a happy place in which to live.

Ashby was a typical small North Lincolnshire village. It had no real character and consisted of one main street with another road at right angles leading to Scunthorpe. It was to this road that we had moved from Crosby. The detached house was next to a decrepit farm owned by a Mr. Hunslett. He worked at the Iron Works and also tended a 2 to 3 acre field where he grew corn or carrots on some form of crop rotation scheme. Mrs Hunslett suffered from epileptic fits and often my mother would rush to look after her when one of the Hunslett children – there were five of them – came round to the house seeking help.

The main street had the usual range of shops: the butchers, the toy shop, the bakers, the Co-op, as well as the village school and the Globe cinema plus the all important fish and chip shop which also sold Tizer in large bottles. We children drank Tizer by the gallon. All the buildings were of the dark red Lincolnshire brick, although the Globe had been painted white with black window frames and black mock beams which tried to give it a Tudor look.

* * * * * * * * * * * * *

The school was small with a triangular front and a small open porch leading into a central hall around which were eight schoolrooms and two cloakrooms, one each for boys and girls. The headmaster's room was at the far end and the teacher's room between two of the smaller classrooms. At the front, behind iron railings and an iron gate, was the playground for the boys, whilst at the side of the school was the girls' playground; the sexes were not allowed to mix. At the other side of the school, there was the bicycle shed and the outside lavatories. Inside the porch was a bell tower with a rope waiting for one of the senior boys to announce that school assembly was only five minutes away. The sound of the bell reverberated across the village and fields and was accepted as part of village life. Punctuality was strict. Any boy who was late for morning assembly was held back in the porch by one of the teachers and was given the cane by the headmaster as soon as he was free. Prayers were said and hymns sung while the whole assembly sat in rows on the wooden floor with the young ones in front.

The cane was the controlling factor in all school activities as far as the boys were concerned, and if the cane was not sufficient to strike terror in all, the headmaster was a fitting accessory. Mr Bramley was of medium height but was solid and on the verge of being fat. He was red faced with black hair and small podgy hands, a bit like a belligerent version of a scaled-down Oliver Hardy. He was a passable piano player and played for all the hymns at assembly. All good piano players had podgy hands according to my mother, who was a mine of rather useless, often biased and generalized information, if it related to Scunthorpe. It seemed to all of us boys that the cane was attached to Mr Bramley and he would use it on any occasion where discipline was seen to be slipping.

If school league tables were based on discipline as well as education, then Ashby Infants School would be near the top of the table. Mr. Bramley would not tolerate any decline in standards either of education or of discipline.

At the age of eleven, all pupils would take two preliminary examinations for entrance either to the Scunthorpe Grammar School or, for the less academic, to the Secondary Modern school and, for the even less fortunate, the general education schools.

Mr. Bramley's aim was to get as many of his pupils into the higher grade of education, and, to this end, he would take charge of all classes in the final year of school. The cane, which was about half an inch thick and about one yard long, took control of the last year's schooling; eyes were hypnotized to its movement through the air until it seemed to develop a life of its own and Mr Bramley seemed merely an adjunct to it. This was the figure of terror that was to invade our lives from the first day of school to the day we left six years later.

Having survived the Carpenter ordeal, life became more routine, although Carpenter had come to the conclusion that I had not learnt the first rule of bullying – that nobody should sneak on the bully – but the cane was there to persuade him to keep him out of mischief.

Mr. Bramley had very quickly discovered that my father was 'something' in the village and, as my father was also a bully, Mr. Bramley, himself a bully, kept clear of him as much as possible. My father's temper was not easy for anyone, least of all for himself, to control. He helped to maintain his status in the village by the fact that he had a car which was uncommon in those pre-war days; it certainly put Mr. Bramley at a disadvantage,

Schooldays were hard to bear. We had to get up at about six thirty; by then my mother would have the fire alight in the living room. There would be a smell of smoke from the coal fire and the smallest, yellowish, flickering flame trying to overcome the coals' attempt to survive unburnt. With the coal would be yesterday's cinders, already having yielded up their heat but still able to make a final attempt to survive another day. The message on all the dustcarts of 'SIFT YOUR CINDERS AND SAVE YOUR RATES' must have impressed my mother because, each day, she would sift the cinders and save all but the dust for the next day.

Sleepy-eyed and still in our pyjamas, my sister Joan and I would crawl downstairs to get washed in front of the fire. An enamel bowl of hot water and a saucer with soap and flannels would be perched on a chair and our hands and faces were wiped around, more to wake us up than remove dirt. An egg each either boiled, poached or scrambled, to start the day, with porridge in winter and Force in the summer.

Then followed a long walk to school and another day keeping out of the way of the cane. The first year was easy, but the future was already being imposed upon us by the continuous, monotonous and mind numbing repetition of multiplication tables. I remember the yearning in the early days of wanting to be in the classes where you could learn tables like the older children. Each class would be reciting its own tables and the result was a drone pervading the air and learning filling the minds.

In the final year, the tables would be over, but the memorizing would continue.

Handwriting was just as important as tables. Letters and words were written out in special notebooks with blue and red lines indicating the size of the letters either in italics or in capitals. Fingers would be put between each letter so that the correct spacing would result. However, notebooks were expensive, so sums and tables were written with hard crayons on slates. Slates could last for years and tests could be erased and started again. This had an added advantage for the pupil in that, with a quick twitch of the elbow, all wrong answers could be rubbed out and a new correct answer put in, before they were marked.

Mr. Bramley's attempt to control cheating and, at the same time, to avoid having to mark books at home in the evenings was partly successful by getting each pupil, having finished his or her test, to pass the slate to the boy or girl next to him or her for marking. This was straight forward ,when tests were given in the classroom, because you had made sure, at the beginning of term, to sit next to your best friend.

Those pupils, who were most likely to get into Scunthorpe Grammar School, were pulled out of the classroom and put into the cloakroom and given test after test day after day but, in spite of all this, the success rate was very poor and only one or two children would pass both the preliminary and final exams. My mother assumed that I would be one of the successful ones, as my sister had been three years earlier.

School started at a quarter to nine with a break at eleven, and morning lessons finished at a quarter to one. Ashby Infants had a large rural catchment area, so many of the children could not get home for lunch and had to take their own lunch to school. My mother would not consider letting me eat with the 'packed-lunchers' and I had to go home each day to have a proper meal. A hot midday meal was as essential just as high tea with jam sandwiches was essential at six o'clock.

School friendships do not last as one moves from school to

school and from home to home, but those friends, made during the first few years of school, play an important part in life. Another very good friend was Alan Cuthbertson, a smallish pink-faced boy who shared hobbies of stamp collecting and playing 'Cowboys and Indians'. Cuthbertson was mild mannered and clever, generally coming top of the class, with me coming second in most cases. In the final year, it was generally taken for granted that we would both go through to the Grammar School. We looked forward to carrying on the friendship for years to come, but fate intervened and just before we were due to take the second entrance exam, Cuthbertson cut his hand badly and was unable to take the exam and consequently failed to get into the Grammar school. Instead, his parents sent him to the Grammar school in Brigg and we only met once more after that.

Some time later, during the following summer holidays, we were both at the Appleby Frodingham sports ground for the visit of the West Indies cricket team who were playing the Minor Counties. The weather was beautiful throughout the match, which was made memorable for me, when Leary Constantine, one of the few black men in the team at that time, seemingly oblivious to what was going on, stood at mid-off with a 'skyer', heading straight down on him and the crowd yelling warnings to him either to get out of the way or catch it. Still with a disinterested look on his face, he moved two paces forward and caught the ball behind his back. That day, Appleby Frodingham was blessed with something rarely seen in any first class ground – brilliant play with a wonderful sense of humour. At the end of the match, Cuthbertson and I were loitering round the back of the main stand trying to get as many autographs as possible on our score cards. We immediately recognized each other, but neither made the first move, we just looked at each other and walked away.

Few school friends remain in one's memory from those early days and then for completely diverse reasons. Alan Cuthbertson lived at the other end of the village with the result that our friendship persisted only in school time.

In the holidays and at weekends, my other friend was, of course, Robinson. To all at school he was 'Owly' Robinson.

His nickname described his looks, he was a pallid, thin child with black hair and a very pale face and wide staring eyes. Owly Robinson sticks in my mind not only because we spent much of our holidays with Smash and Grab going for walks in the country, but for two other particularly traumatic reasons, both of which resulted in him getting three strokes of the cane.

The first occasion took place in the school hall, which had a stage at one end. Whilst milling around one morning waiting for assembly and the daily hand and boot inspection, Owly stuck his finger in an electric light socket on the front edge of the stage, which would, when school concerts or prize-giving, occurred, be used for the footlights. Owly was instantly hit with 240 volts. He staggered a couple of steps and flopped to the floor. For a moment, Owly had the reaction-time of a dinosaur; it took him several seconds to realize what he had done and try to respond. Boot inspection was due any minute and that was uppermost in his mind. He struggled to his feet too late to outwit Mr. Bramley who intimidated the truth out of one of the juniors. No fear of court actions or compensation entered Mr. Bramley's mind. No fear of Health and Safety Officers. No fear of irate parents. Just the Bramley 'justice system' for a rule breaker, three strokes of the cane on the right hand and back to your row, possibly the best way of getting over an electric shock, far quicker than the routine cup of weak tea.

There was no real sympathy from his classmates; any show of sympathy would be treated as treason with the standard response of three strokes.

To be honest, Owly was not very bright and was often picked upon by the headmaster, not with the intention of improving his knowledge, but more as a bit of light relief from the usual earnest answers of the brighter pupils.

In a general knowledge lesson and quiz, for general knowledge was part of the entrance exams to the Grammar School, Mr. Bramley asked Owly to describe a sphere. Owly gave, what to him was a rapid and plausible answer. "A sphere" he said, with supreme confidence, "is a long stick with a point on the end". If Owly was capable of a smug grin, he would have given it then, for the first time in his school history, he had answered quickly and, as he thought, correctly. He had stunned the class into a shocked silence. The half of the class that knew a sphere was not a long stick with a point on the end was silent; they guessed the fate that would befall Robinson. The other half was stunned that, for once, Owly had responded immediately with an answer that not only impressed them, but would surely impress Mr. Bramley.

Owly was shaken to the core, when confronted with a berserk Mr. Bramley who, for some reason, thought he was being 'got at' or perhaps he just felt like an outburst of temper. He charged across the room waving his cane and knocking over the blackboard and easel. He dragged the poor child out to the front of the class by his left ear and gave him three of the best, as usual, on the hand. Owly was stunned by his change of fortune from hero one minute to villain the next. I never knew whether anybody ever explained to Owly where he had gone wrong. At the time, we were too frightened by Mr Bramley's outburst of temper that we just froze like statues.

Claridge was another boy, who remains as a vivid memory, not that I was ever a friend of his. Certainly, if I had been shown any sign of friendship, my mother would have been up to the school at top speed. Ashby Infants School with its large rural situation included a few gypsy caravans parked on the outskirts of the village. Truancy was not a problem, as the School Inspectors were always on the prowl, but even they had difficulty in keeping up with the gypsies. Perhaps Claridge was not a real gypsy, as he was fair-haired, but he was an irregular school pupil and was thus a rule breaker in Mr. Bramley's eyes. Rule breakers were bread and butter to him. Claridge had a rough time in school, but probably had a rougher time at home; he always had red-rimmed eyes, caked with sleep, and one assumed he had been crying. He always seemed to have a cold and a runny nose and, if he had anything to wipe it with, it would be a dirty old rag. Mr. Bramley could sense Claridge's presence, even if he could not see him. At one assembly, he realised that Claridge had arrived late and was being held in the porch for punishment. Assembly was stopped! Mr. Bramley stormed through the children sitting on the floor and dragged

Claridge, already crying, to the front and onto the stage. Even a headmaster, as experienced with rural children as he was, seemed to be taken aback by Claridge's general appearance and particularly with his runny nose made worse by the floods of tears already flowing. Clenching his cane even more fiercely, he grabbed the boy by the right ear and dragged him back through the shocked assembly to the front door and forced the yelling Claridge to wipe his nose on the front door mat. The rough coconut matting on a sore nose was just what Claridge did not want.

The whole school was stunned for the rest of the day.

The reign of terror, however, never had a hundred percent success. The younger brother of Thompson, a boy in my class, was a rebel. He was always in trouble and yet never succumbed to Bramley's tyranny. I saw little of him, but always recall him being dragged through the hall by his right ear, whilst hacking with his boots at the headmaster's legs as he went. No doubt, young Thompson lost, but he remained somewhat of a hero throughout his infant days. However, he was too dangerous to make friends with.

Tragedy struck in the final year as the father of one of the boy's died. Harvey was the name of the family, and they kept the local sweet shop, but not the one that we Ablett's went to, as it was a bit down-market according to my mother. She always used the one on the main road, which was run by Mrs Welch who was also a relief teacher at the school and thus more acceptable. We had no idea of what to say to a boy who had lost his father, so the whole class did the obvious thing and said nothing. Harvey would spend the break-time sitting alone on his haunches in a corner of the playground. This self-imposed isolation continued until the end of term, when the holidays removed the problem as far as we were concerned.

Girls were not really a part of our life. They shared the classroom but not the playground or Mr Bramley's cane. They sat on one side of the classroom with the boys on the other. They never seemed to be a challenge either to Cuthbertson or myself at the end of term or end of year exams. The boys at Ashby Infants School were not into fraternizing with girls, who were considered inferior. The girls were not quite so insular and the occasional crush would emerge and when it happened to me, it was not quite so unwelcome as it should have been. Her name was Helena and she was tall, thin and dark haired and pale, as most children were in that part of the world, partly due to the post war recession and partly to the Lincolnshire climate of cold easterly winds and the lack of hot sun at any time of the year. Even so, Helena had slightly rosy cheeks, making her doll-like. She made it plain that she liked me by standing beside me whenever there was the chance, but we talked very little and then only on school subjects. Nevertheless, I demonstrated my desirability by sitting at my desk with my left arm overhanging the back of the seat, showing off my wristwatch: we sat in double desks, which I shared with Cuthbertson. I was the only boy with a wristwatch in the final year and for this I was of some interest to the opposite sex. Not only that, I was made the 'time' prefect, which involved leaving the classroom at the end of each half hour and going into the hall and ringing a hand bell announcing the time for subjects to change. The affair with Helena progressed no further than this and ended when we moved to other schools.

* * * * * * * * * * * * * *

Where classes eliminated any individuality, playtime brought out the best or the worst in us. Life became competitive. The common currency was either cigarette cards or marbles. Cigarette card collecting was very popular as most fathers smoked, either Players, Woodbine or Capstan. New series of cards were published at frequent intervals and the rush was on immediately a new series came out to try to finish the old series with a complete set. Albums could be obtained by writing directly to the Cigarette Company. 'English and Australian Cricket Players' was a very popular set as was 'Weapons of the World'. But perhaps the most popular was a set dealing with torture throughout the ages.

This was the non-physical aspect of cigarette cards – collecting, swapping, sticking in albums and always trying to get a set of cards in pristine condition.

The physical side of card collecting was truly competitive. The most common game was to place a card upright, leaning it against the playground wall. Then two or more boys would take it in turn to flick their cards from a specified distance at the card leaning against the wall until it was knocked down. The boy who succeeded in knocking it down would then become the owner of all the 'failed' cards. Each boy would possessively carry around a huge bunch of cards held together with a rubber band. Each bundle of cards would contain one or more favourite cards, which would have some imagined, mystical power and therefore be ready to be drawn out of the pack, once the risk of losing another 'special' loomed.

Marbles were more of an entrepreneurial occupation, because there were known winners and losers. The game was played with clay marbles, which could be bought by the dozen from the local sweet shop or toy-shop, at a very low price. Again, the game was to hit a target marble and win all the failed ones. To the ordinary boy it was as risky as cigarette cards. Perhaps some of my father's go-ahead spirit was passed on to me, as it was not long before I realized that greed was a weakness in most boys – I made a decision to capitalize on this greed. With a fret saw I cut five little arches, just bigger than a marble, in a piece of plywood, stuck two supports at the back to prop it up, and printed 1, 3, 5, 4 and 2 over the arches in that order, and set up my stand in front of the school wall. It was an immediate success, particularly with those boys running out of marbles who saw the chance of getting five back if the aim was good. I started raking in the marbles at quite an astonishing rate – even so, the occasional paying out the odd five marbles to a chance winner rankled, especially as some of the boys seemed to have quite a good aim. Winnings began to drop. Reducing the size of the holes was not on, as a new board would be immediately recognized with a subsequent loss of goodwill. I worked mainly with Cuthbertson and sent him off on a new plan. He did a quick 'recce' around the playground and soon found a new site to set up the board, this time behind a slight but not obvious ridge in the tarmac – the trick worked; suddenly those, who had been hitting the '5' all too frequently in the past, found their aim faltering, but pride and a reputation of being an expert kept them plugging away, even when they were losing more often than winning. My store of marbles grew at a quick rate.

Glass marbles, or 'taws' as we called them, were more expensive and used in games only on rare occasions.

These special marbles were only used in long-range games, which were not suitable for playgrounds. Returning home from school gave us the opportunity to use them and they would be thrown along the gutter by the side of the road, carefully avoiding the grating where they could be easily lost. The aim was to hit the opponent's marble in front and then, if a hit was made, take possession of his marble. This reached a sudden end for me one evening whilst heading home for tea, as it seems I was nearly hit by a lorry, all observed by Mr. Bramley, who happened to be passing at the time.

The next morning at assembly, the Headmaster announced that he had seen a stupid boy nearly getting run over the previous evening. I knew that if it had not been for the fear of my father's temper, Mr. Bramley would have had me out at the front for a beating. The warning had been given, however, and the game ceased from that time.

Each year, the steel works held a day's outing to Cleethorpes and all the school children would be herded onto buses and shipped out for the day.

Although the depression was over and most men had a job, wages were low and families were large. Summer holidays were too expensive for most families. The day's outing was all the holiday that most children had. All the local junior schools were invited and all children could go, whether or not their fathers worked in the iron or steel works. This was the only free outing for most of my school, but not for me, as my mother would not have me go to Cleethorpes with the other ruffians. So I stayed at home and looked out of the bedroom window and watched the buses heading through Ashby for a day at the seaside. I cannot remember any real regret for not joining my school mates, perhaps because I feared that, out of sight of the teachers, Carpenter might have seen his one chance of revenge.

Due to Mr. Bramley's pressure and the help of my mother, I made it to the Grammar School, but poor old Owly didn't even get to the Secondary Modern. We moved house and Owly and I lost contact with each other.

* * * * * * * * * * * * *

The Grammar School was quite modern; it had two quadrangles with classrooms set evenly around them. I managed to stay in the top class at the end of each year, mainly due to the good work of my sister, who was much more clever than I was. The cane was only used sparingly and then only for some exceptional misdeed. As usual, the girls were separated from the boys in the classroom and in the playground and playing fields. Life was quite good, but bullying was still quite common, mainly by the teachers.

By this time, Smash and Grab had succumbed to distemper, but experience had taught my mother that nursing such a messy disease was unlikely to be successful and they were put down in the early stages of the infection.

Once again, my reward for getting to the Grammar school was a puppy. There is no better present for a child than a kitten or a puppy and the new one was the ideal. He was a Labrador and had the Labrador's traits of taking two years to grow up. He developed into a deep-chested brute of a dog, which would not tolerate too much discipline. He was immediately named 'Pongo' and was fearless. He would fight any dog approaching the front garden and was also particularly antagonistic towards the coalman. The coalman had a somewhat frightening appearance as he had, at some time, and probably in the war, lost his right hand which was replace by a metal hook: this had the advantage in that he could use the hook to claw into the coal sack and heave it onto his back. .Although fearless in most aspects of his life, we found that Pongo had one or two chinks in his armour. He was frightened of thunder and would hide under the kitchen table when storms approached; this gave us the opportunity of capitalizing on this fear by keeping a sheet of metal near the backdoor – my mother only had to rattle it and he would run in and hide. I believe Thurber had a similar dog.

It is often said that dogs and cats have a sixth sense and can forecast the approach of a thunderstorm and rain. Many years later, I was able to dispute this 'sixth-sense' theory. We had a Dandie Dinmont bitch called 'Pepper' who would hide under the settee and salivate profusely when a storm was approaching. As she got older, she became very deaf and her ability to forecast thunder was lost. It would seem that dogs and cats have a much more acute sense of hearing than we have and hear the thunder long before we humans do.

Pongo was also afraid of the sound of our 'cap guns', and I am sorry to say I often played on this fear when he was being obstinate. My love of dogs must have been inherited, because it seemed my parents were always happy to add another dog to the family.

For some reason, when Pongo was about three years old, my father decided to bring another pup into the house and this time it was a Dachshund. We named him 'Korki'. He turned out to be quite stupid and quickly settled into the family, deciding that his sleeping area would be in front of the coal fire inside the fender. Even though he suffered burns on several occasions from burning coals falling from the grate, he never seemed to be deterred by these mishaps and would immediately return to his 'bed' as soon as his burnt stomach had been bandaged with a swab of cold tea.

The arrival of Korki had an astounding effect on Pongo. The fierce Labrador suddenly became the timid Labrador when confronted with the minute Dachshund pup. Korki would demand to sit or lay wherever Pongo had settled and Pongo would immediately move and find another chair to sit on.

Within a year, Pongo developed what I would now call 'wet eczema' and was taken to the nearest vet in Gainsborough. My father returned later, somewhat shaken, without Pongo; he had been told that the condition was incurable. In retrospect, I believe that the eczema problem was merely due to fleas, but Pongo had been 'put down'. All of the family, including Korki experienced a gap in our lives for some time.

I obtained the required number of 'O' levels to get into the Sixth form, but this coincided with my father suddenly and quite unexpectedly leaving us for another woman. I never saw him again and he seemed never to want to see any of us again. Korki was given to a neighbour and we moved to Nottingham. At last, my mother escaped from Scunthorpe, but not in the circumstances that she had hoped for.

My two Sixth Form years were spent at The High Pavement School in Nottingham. The teaching was excellent and the teachers became admired human beings and not bullies.

Mr. Thrasher was our Physics teacher and my housemaster, he was tall, hook-nosed, but interested in his pupils. His name belied his temperament. His assistant was not quite so amiable, but we saw little of him. He was a Rhodes scholar, which impressed us, although we did not know what it meant. He had one habit, which would appal the modern teaching profession: he would take his class smoking a cigarette. This, in itself, was unique, but what was even more so was the fact that he was able to give his lessons with the cigarette dangling from his lower lip. We never found out how he was able to keep it stuck to his lip, even when talking, but it gave us something to look at, when he was giving a boring lesson.

Our Chemistry teacher was a Mr. Morrison, younger than Mr. Thrasher, who went to great lengths to help us and was always at hand to explain problems. We found out that he was keen on politics and was 'high up' in the Commonwealth Party. On several occasions, our Chemistry class – there were only four of us – went to his political meetings. I never knew what became of the Commonwealth Party, but it seemed to die a death somewhere along the line. Mr. Morrison showed his fondness for his students; on one particular occasion, when one of the class had been dragged along the bench by his feet in some boyish prank, and had grabbed a water tap which extended upwards from a sink, and had pulled it from its junction to the mains with the result that the lab was flooded, Mr. Morrison explained to the headmaster, a Mr. Potter, that there was a corroded junction and that the pipe had given way during normal use.

Our Botany classes were given by a young Irish teacher, by the name of Miss Looney. An unfortunate name, which resulted in her suffering a certain amount of chiding, but we all admired her for her knowledge and helpfulness and her ability to accept our rude comments on her name.

Miss McKenzie, a severe woman, taught us Zoology. She did not like me, so in consequence, I did not like her. Under her instruction, we did our dissection of a cockroach and a rock salmon [an elite name for a dogfish] and stretched out a dead earthworm on a card and opened that up as part of the 'A' level requirement.

The 'A' level results were good, and I was accepted as a second year student at the Royal Veterinary College, London.

On the whole, I was happy at High Pavement, even though it was an old, multi-story red brick building with cold concrete stairs and no playing fields. We had to travel by bus every Wednesday afternoon in the winter, for either rugby or cross-country running, both of which I hated. In the summer, we played cricket on the 'Forest', an area of parkland not far from the centre of Nottingham.

My sister and I survived the absence of a father, mainly by being preoccupied with tending a mother who seemed to be perpetually crying. But, as time went by, home-life quietened down and my dream was showing signs of coming to fruition. In a few weeks, I would be heading for College, but not to the massive red brick building in Royal College Street in London, but to Reading University's main building near the centre of the town to where the first two years of the Vet's course had been evacuated.

* * * * * * * * * * * * *

The war had started when I was at Scunthorpe, but seemed to have had little effect on our lives. I was too young to be 'called up' and we all expected that Germany would have collapsed within a few weeks; when it didn't, we just carried on.

Air raid shelters had to be built at the schools in case raids took place in school hours. Until they were completed, we had to attend school for half a day each week to be given homework on each subject. This gave me the opportunity of getting my sister to do my homework and, in so doing, I was considered to be a very bright pupil. Of course, my 'undoing' came when work was done 'in class' and my intelligence status declined rapidly.

Bombing was more common in Nottingham than in Scunthorpe but still had no long-lasting effect on my life. Money was scarce and my mother managed to get a job in the Tax Office and, at that time I never really appreciated all that she did for us.

College beckoned and a new life was starting.

STUDENT DAYS
"Much study is a weariness of the flesh"
Ecclesiastes

CHAPTER II

STUDENT DAYS

Qualification was not a dramatic move from freedom to responsibility. In those days, students were required to 'see practice' in their holidays and this was not merely travelling with the practice vet to learn the problems of diagnosis and treatment, but, in the eyes of the unscrupulous vet, to act as an unpaid assistant.

The war was dragging on and our anticipation of a quick and satisfactory end was shattered by the dramatic reversal of fortune and the drama of Dunkerque. Conscription was postponed until our college days were over or earlier, if we failed our annual examinations. Even so, we had to enrol in the Officers' Training Corps with its weekly square bashing and five mile walks. Holidays were no relief as we were required to join the local Home Guard in whichever town we were 'seeing practice'.

* * * * * * * * * * * * *

Over the years, students had built up a list of good practices to go to and those which were either antagonistic to students or which arranged poor living accommodation and the minimum of help.

My first experience was in a practice in Bedford. Bedford, in those days, was not the attractive bustling town that it is now; it was quiet and rather refined and was described to me by another student as a 'cemetery with traffic lights'. I had an aunt and uncle living in the town, which was probably the main reason why I chose to go to the practice there. No fellow student recommended it, so I had no real idea what I was letting myself in for. I do not recall seeing much of my aunt or uncle, as it so happened that the owner of the practice, who worked single-handed with a very efficient secretary, decided to go on a week's holiday two days after I arrived.

I had started college as a second year student in September, [having been excused the first year due to my good Higher School Certificate results] and my stay in Bedford was at the beginning of the Christmas holidays – I had only been at college for about ten weeks and by then had only been taught the basics of biochemistry and physiology. It is worth reminding the reader that the war was still raging; people were having to deal with the trauma that was affecting every person's life in one way or another. There was no counselling or self-pity and every effort that one made was appreciated. There was never any thought of suing or legal action and students were given freedom to carry on as best they could. Even so, I doubt whether a student with ten weeks' training and acting as a professional would have been tolerated by 'The Royal College'.

My accommodation was a boarding house near the centre of Bedford and now, in retrospect, and then being naïve, I think that the man running it was gay, as he had two rather effeminate young men boarding with him. On my first night at these 'digs' I was asked whether I wanted to share a bedroom with him or have my own room. An odd question to an eighteen year old who was brought up in Ashby where 'gay' meant being happy and the word 'homosexual' would have been meaningless.

I survived that experience by choosing my own room. More importantly, my life depended, at that time, on my prayers that no difficult cases would turn up. Fortunately, there were no bad calvings to attend and the farmers that I saw were friendly and helpful. I survived on the words given to us by our Professor of Medicine, Professor Burrows, before the finals.

"Gentlemen", he said, "never forget that 90% of your cases will recover in spite of your treatment".

How right he was!

I recall the only real problem that I had was due to my own stupidity.

A lady brought in an old mongrel bitch with ulcerating mammary tumours and she expected quick treatment. I learned later that the Veterinary Surgeon had been delaying any surgery, as the tumour was quite extensive. I felt that I should do my best for the dog, and the owner, and I decided to operate the next day. I spent the evening looking up every aspect of surgery in every textbook that I could find. The secretary was marvellous, she told me how to give the anaesthetic [I used a local, as I did not fancy giving a general anaesthetic at the same time as operating]. I carefully dissected out the tumour. The poor dog showed no sign of pain, possibly because I gave it too much of the local anaesthetic. Local anaesthesia depends on injecting the anaesthetic all the way round where the scalpel is to be used. After suturing the wound, which was about six inches long, the secretary and I bandaged it up and sent the patient home with a rather artistic cummerbund, which was already becoming stained with blood. The operation was, by its very nature, 'bloody', as tumours become well supplied with blood vessels. The animal survived and was quite cheerful when it sat on the table a week later to have its stitches removed; it even wagged its tail when it saw me! The owner was happy and paid the bill of thirty shillings quite readily. I did not receive any thanks from the vet on his return from holiday but did get £2.00 when I finally left on Christmas Eve. I was much cheaper than a locum.

That experience always brings to mind a cartoon in the Journal of the American Veterinary Medical Association some years ago, which showed two parallel drawings of a veterinary surgeon operating on a cat. The drawings were in the form of children's paintings, where the picture was divided into numbered sections for the child to paint in the appropriate colours.

The first drawing had the caption: "This is a drawing of a veterinarian trying to spay a tom cat. Paint the veterinarian's face red and leave the rest of the painting white".

The second was exactly the same with the caption: "This is a drawing of a veterinarian accidentally cutting the carotid artery. Leave the veterinarian's face white and colour the rest of the picture red". I know what he meant.

That particular practice was next door to a public house and the Vet spent most evenings swilling beer and playing darts. In the few days that we were together in the practice, he decided that we should be a 'team' and it turned out that the two of us were unbeatable after a few beers. I was never a good darts player, but it seemed that, after a pint or two, my aim improved. The result was, that, after each successful game, the losing team bought drinks for the winners with the outcome that we drank too much. The Vet was a heavy drinker anyway and drank his pints at a much faster pace than I did. If an urgent call came through in the evening, his wife would pop in from the house next door and call us out. She did her own drinking at home and was often seen at the 'jug and bottle' window, replenishing her own supply of beer in a jug.

When we did go out to a farm at night and during drinking time, it was left to me the next morning to try and explain the location and treatment given the night before, as the vet would have forgotten where we had been and what he had done. His veterinary ability simulated his dart's ability; it appeared to improve with the intake of beer.

That particular practice did teach me something: one could get by with the minimum of drugs. The small-animal pharmacy consisted of four jars of aspirin tablets, coloured white, pink, yellow and mauve. There was also one large bottle of 'Air-Raid' mixture, consisting of a solution of potassium bromide, which was a sedative and was commonly used to calm dogs when they were nervous. It was also the only medicine for dogs, which were suffering from fits in the later stages of distemper. Distemper was still rife everywhere and there was no cure for it. Vaccines were twenty years away and distemper was a killer. As to aspirin tablets, they are gastric irritants and dogs are very 'vomit prone'. In spite of this, I met clients who would swear, for example, that the yellow tablets were far better than the mauve ones and would demand what colour tablets they needed. With the absence of antibiotics and chemotherapeutics, one had to treat symptoms rather than the disease. I wonder how much knowledge of nursing has been lost now that so many specific therapies are available.

Before I left, I spent the £2.00 on Christmas presents for my mother and sister and went home happy that I had survived the experience unscathed.

I never went back to the Bedford practice, but did have the satisfaction of returning to college in the following January to boast to the other students of my operating skills.

* * * * * * * * * * * * *

In the summer holidays, I went to see practice in Goldhawk Road, Shepherd's Bush in London. This was not a horse practice but dealt only with dogs and cats and other sundry pets. The senior partner was a Mr. Gerald Broad who had a cousin, Mr. Stanley Broad, who had another veterinary practice in Lancaster Gate, much closer to the West End of London.

But this was a 'heavy horse' practice and later had a lasting impression on me. Mr. Gerald Broad was instrumental in getting me my first assistantship at his cousin's practice. In later college holidays, I spent my time at the Lancaster Gate practice.

Mr. Gerald Broad and his wife were very gentle people, kind and helpful. I was given a room and had all my meals with the family. There seemed to be little space available in the house from which the practice was run, because the waiting room was also used as the consulting room. This meant that the very large table in the centre was used by both the Veterinary Surgeons in the practice, Mr Gerald Broad and his assistant, Miss Woodger, at the same time. When I was there, there were three of us, each with a corner, examining different animals. I was given a free hand and never recall that either of the Veterinary Surgeons interfered with my diagnosis or treatment, but I did not do any house visits or operations on my own.

At surgery time, the place was pandemonium. One has only to imagine the problems that arose when a dog and, for example, two cats were on the table together, encouraged by the audience of dogs sitting with their owners awaiting their turn. A secretary sat at a desk nearby, taking pence, shillings and half-crowns when the consultation was over.

On the whole, surgery hours passed without too many problems, although I do remember one woman, whose cat was in a wicker basket, decided that her cat was getting nervous with all the barking dogs and she took it out of the basket to nurse it. The cat went berserk, jumped onto the woman's head, dug its claws into her scalp and died. Somehow we managed to prise the cat's claws from her flesh and took it away for cremation – the owner was not charged.

One learnt a little psychology from the experience gained at that practice. If we were confronted by awkward clients, there was a technique for dealing with them. Awkward clients can damage one's reputation, as they tend to make their dissatisfaction public and generally complain in an extra loud voice. The answer was simple, point out in a similarly loud voice that their animal had, in some way, been neglected. For cats, the response was to imply that the cats had fleas. This was generally true anyway, as most London cats had fleas and the modern insecticides had not been invented. For dogs, bad ears or, in long coated dogs, knotted fur were demonstrated in a derogatory voice, with the result that the audience of waiting clients would mutter to each other that the owner must have been very negligent to leave his, or generally her, pet in such a disgraceful state.

Those were happy holidays, especially as I became fond of one of the kennel-maids and went to the Proms with her on several occasions. However, the friendship waned, once I was back in College.

Later, I joined the Lancaster Gate practice of Mr Stanley Broad as a student and started to learn about 'heavy horses'.

* * * * * * * * * * * * * *

After my year in Reading, which was the College second year, the third year was spent in the Thames-side village of Sonning and this was near enough to Reading to allow me to carry on staying at my 'digs' there. After that we went off to Streatley for our final two years.

On the whole, life in College was quite good. These final two years were spent at Streatley House. Lectures were held in a large wooden shed, which had the advantage of being equipped with a table tennis table, a favourite sport in the winter months.

Some of the lecturers and professors were insignificant, whilst others left a lasting impression.

Our professor in Embryology and Histology was Professor Amoroso. He was a large man, highly qualified; he was a medical doctor and later became a Fellow of the Royal Society, a very prestigious honour. He was dark-skinned and either had a glass eye or a severe cast in one eye, which made it very difficult for students to know who he was questioning, but, he was very kind and a brilliant teacher.

Sometimes, it is an advantage to have a name beginning with 'Ab', and this advantage was demonstrated in Professor Amoroso's case.

It was always my policy, in any lecture, to sit at the back and keep a low profile on the presumption that the lecturer would not know how ignorant I was of the subject in question.

Before the exams, we would have 'grinds', [revision classes], to prime us for the forthcoming exams. I recall, as the embryology exam approached, I decided that I must do some revision in the evenings, and one night settled down to learn the pathway of the eighth cranial nerve; I made notes hoping that a question on this topic would turn up in the exam.

The next morning, Professor Amoroso decided to go through the eighth cranial nerve with the class. His first question was where the nerve left the brain and what foramen it went through in the cranium. He asked the class to answer the first question and no-one volunteered any answer. The professor decided to question each of us in turn, and, looking at the register, gazed round the room with his one good eye, asked where Ablett was. As usual, I was at the back and was asked to stand up and give an answer. In the circumstances, I was able to describe the whole pathway, which impressed the Professor and the whole class.

A week later, I was ushered into the exam room and placed in front of a microscope with a pile of slides to look at. I was, of course, first to be examined. I sat down at the laboratory bench beside the examining professor, who had come over from Ireland. I was ready to start by describing slide number one. Before I could start, however, Professor Amoroso walked in and shook hands with the examiner, who he had not met for some years. He leaned over, as I was peering down the microscope, put his arm round my shoulder and said to the examiner:

"Don't worry about Ablett, he is one of my best students". With that comment, they went off for coffee and that was the end of my examination!

However, the 'Ab' prefix had its disadvantages too, which occurred the following year. As usual, I was the first into the practical 'meat-inspection' exam.

'Meat Inspection' was not my subject and, other than two or three lectures and a visit to an abattoir in Reading, there was no further teaching.

The examination was set in a barn and, first as usual, I was confronted with an exhibition of various bits of meat to identify. They were laid out on two wooden doors placed on four trestles. One lump of flesh was pointed out to me to identify. I was mystified and gazed at it.

"What is that?" the examiner asked.

I had no idea; it was a complete mystery to me. In order to say something, I started to tell him what it was not.

"Its not brain", I said, "Not lung, not pancreas, not liver, not kidney, not stomach".

"But what is it?" he asked.

After some time, which seemed like hours, he realised he was not going to get an answer, so out of humanity, gave me a clue.

"What do they keep cows for?" he asked.

"For beef", I said,

"And what else?" he asked with a hint of impatience.

"For producing calves for veal", I volunteered.

He gave up.

I gave up and he gave me the answer.

"It is a piece of the udder", he said. "They keep cows for milk". His tone was now derisory.

"That's enough", he remarked pointing to the door.

"I will see you at Christmas".

This was a direct statement that I had failed.

If the lump had been shown to me with a piece of skin on it, I might have been able to answer, but I had never seen a piece of the inside of an udder before.

Fortunately, I did well enough in the other fourth year exams to negate the meat inspection catastrophe. At least, I was able to alert the other students on one exhibit.

The other professor that comes to mind was Professor Jimmy McCunn. He was professor of Anatomy, a veterinary surgeon, a medical doctor and an obstetrician. He was portly, about 60 years old, always in a suit with a waistcoat and a gold pocket watch and chain. Professor McCunn was a kindly man and always ready to help the 'student in trouble'. He had a keen sense of humour and a ready wit.

The horse was the main animal for study in the forties and most lectures were related to horse diseases and ailments. We dissected a horse and were examined mainly on horse anatomy. In one lecture, I recall him standing on the rostrum, holding up a scapula bone and asking one of the students [known to be a bit of an idler], "What is that?"

The student woke from his reverie and answered: "Yes, sir".

"What do you mean, Yes sir? I asked you what it was. Is it a scapula of a cow or a horse?"

"I'm sorry sir", said the student: "I was misconceived".

"You weren't misconceived", said the Professor. "You were miscarried".

I was to meet up with Professor McCunn later when in practice.

During our third year, when we were studying anatomy, we were obviously impressed that, at last, we were getting closer to real veterinary work, and the dissection classes gave us an added impetus to learn as much as we could on the structure of the animal.

This impression must have been stimulated even more by the Professor's enthusiasm. That proves that a good teacher brings out the best in his pupils.

At that time, I was sharing 'digs' with a fellow student, David Barnett, in a large Victorian House in Reading, close to Prospect Park. I had a room at the front and David a room at the back. The house was owned by Mr. and Mrs. Bolton; they had one daughter. They also had a large black mongrel dog, called Brutus.

The Bolton's were middle-aged, very charming people with a lively sense of humour. The daughter was in her early twenties, with a very pallid complexion and black hair swept back from her forehead. She did no work, but spent most of her time playing the piano and looking sad. I think she was seeing herself as either Greta Garbo or Violetta in La Traviata or, most probably, a mixture of the two.

On the whole, it was a cheerful family, and both David and I spent happy terms there.

During the summer term, David and I decided to improve our anatomical skills by doing a little home dissection.

How we ever came to the decision to try and sneak a dead animal into the house to dissect, I will never know, but students do crazy things. We realised that the animal must be reasonably small, but we had no access to a dead dog or cat. In the end, we went to the abattoir, where we had previously spent one hour studying meat inspection and obtained a premature calf, probably from a cow that had been taken in as a casualty.

This calf was about the size of an Airedale terrier, but was limp and easy to get into a sack.

We managed to get it into David's room without being disturbed and we removed the bottom drawer of his chest of drawers, turned it upside down, covered it with newspaper and lay the calf on it. We were ready to start. Each of us had our own dissection kit, forceps, scalpel, tweezers and needle. We opened our anatomy book and started.

This was on a Thursday in the middle of June and during a heat wave.

By Friday morning, there was a whiff of flesh in the room, but not too overpowering.

Unfortunately, after Friday's lessons, David decided to go home to Balham for the weekend, probably to avoid sleeping with the corpse, but not before returning to the digs to collect his clothes.

We were able to lock our rooms, so that nobody could see the carcass laid out on the newspaper and covered with the sack. We considered our plan of action and came to the conclusion that David should lock his room and leave the window open to allow fresh air in. I was to keep away from the room, as it would be suspicious, if Mr. or Mrs. Bolton were to see me near David's room. Anyway I did not have a key.

David was to return on Sunday evening and we would carry on from there.

Saturday was a scorcher and I spent most of the day

in a fairground in the park. It would have been impossible to work, as the fairground was blaring out loud music until eleven or twelve o'clock at night, not only that, the music was repetitive with "Lay that Pistol Down Babe", transmitted over a loudspeaker, every two or three minutes.

I went back to the house in the early evening of Saturday for the evening meal and, over the main course, Mrs. Butler remarked that Brutus was missing David. Apparently, he was sitting outside David's door, refusing to come down for his dinner.

Until then, Brutus had enjoyed our company, as we often took him into the park and threw balls and sticks for him to retrieve.

"He's very fond of David", I said, "I expect he will be very pleased to see him come back. I'll take him for a walk after dinner".

I went upstairs and there was Brutus sitting by the door with an occasional sniff at the crack at the bottom of the door.

Dogs' noses are very sensitive, but I thought that even my nose could pick up an unpleasant smell. I had to drag Brutus from his vigil and we went for a walk. Dogs have good memories, and as soon as we got home, he made a beeline for David's room.

Fortunately, it was at the end of the corridor, so not too obvious that unpleasant smells were coming from it. The next morning, it became a talking point over breakfast. Brutus was definitely pining for David and how much he must love him.

"Never mind", I said, "David will be home this evening and Brutus will be happy again".

I took him for another walk, but this time he was even more reluctant to go and pulled heartily to get back home.

By then, the smell was becoming quite obvious, but perhaps more so to me because I was anticipating it. I wanted David back as soon as possible, as I had no access to his bedroom and things were getting desperate. I had no telephone number to call him to urge him to get an early train. I dreaded the thought that he might delay his return until the following day.

The day was getting hotter and the scent of rotting meat might be attractive to a dog but it scared the daylights out of me and it seemed to be getting stronger. I decided to go to Reading

Station and await David, although I had no idea what train he would be on. By being there, I felt that I was half a step nearer to solving the problem. Not only that, I was away from the house and possible inquisition.

In due course, David arrived and I grabbed him.

On the way to our 'digs', I told him the story as to what had happened; that Brutus was going mad and that the smell was becoming quite noticeable. We decided that we must get rid of the corpse immediately but, in the euphoria of having got it, we had failed to consider how to get rid of it.

We got back to the house in what we hoped was a nonchalant air and went up to David's room. Brutus was still there and got even more excited than normal when he realized that we were going in – he wanted to rush in first and relish the feast that he imagined was awaiting him. I hauled him back and David opened the door.

A buzz went up and what seemed like thousands of bluebottles erupted from the carcass like a black cloud. Brutus was barking outside, so I opened the door to quieten him and grabbed his collar. The flesh of the dead body was dotted with masses of cream coloured specks, which were bluebottle eggs. The whole room was full of flies and they were beginning to find their way into the landing. This meant that we had to slam the door closed as quickly as possible and think of some way of getting rid of the carcass and the flies.

We came up with the idea that we would try and bury it in Mr. Bolton's allotment. The idea was good, he kept spades and forks in a shed in the garden but we were handicapped by it being midsummer and the sun did not set until nearly eleven.

"We are taking Brutus for a walk", we told the Boltons.

"It's cool now and he could do with the exercise".

Our bicycles were in the garden near the shed, so getting the garden tools was not a problem. We waited until the family was listening to the news on the wireless and sneaked out with the body in its sack. There was no need to entice Brutus to come with us, he was having the time of his life and still imagined he would have the opportunity to savour the carcass.

We went to the allotment, found a bit of land that looked recently dug over, quickly dug a shallow grave and buried the body.

Brutus immediately started to 'unbury' it, but we managed to drag him away. He rarely accompanied Mr. Bolton on his gardening visits, so we felt reasonably assured that we would be safe for a while and maybe even up to the summer holidays, which were only two weeks away.

The next morning was somewhat of an ordeal, and we waited for any comments.

"Brutus seems to have settled down now that you are back, David. He missed you very much and sat by your door all day", remarked Mrs Bolton over breakfast.

"He likes his walks", replied David. "We'll take him again tonight".

"By the way", Mrs. Boltpn said to her husband, "there seem to be swarms of flies about. This hot weather must have brought them out. Do you think it was due to all the litter that the Fairground people left behind, when they moved on last night?"

"Most probably", said Mr. Bolton. "Those people should be reported – it's very unhealthy".

Two weeks later, we left and prepared for our forth year in Streatley. We sent Christmas cards to the Boltons that year, but by then we had moved on.

Did Mr Bolton discover the body?

Did that piece of land produce bumper crops?

Did Brutus decide he liked visiting the allotment with Mr. Bolton?

We shall never know, but I feel sure that David and I were never accused of burying a carcass in the allotment, even if it had been discovered; we were too nice for that. Most probably, the fairground men would be blamed and had to suffer slanderous accusations.

During term time, students either 'lived-in' at the College in dormitories, or in 'digs'. Living in 'digs' gave one some privacy, but there were disadvantages. Travelling to College was one difficulty and particularly during cold and snowy winters, and loss of companionship was another. But living in digs had its advantages. The main meal of the day was in the College dining rooms but, with the severe food and fuel rationing, it was possible to take advantage of both sources, as most landladies managed some hot food when we arrived back 'home' in a frozen state.

My very first landlady in Reading was a young married woman with two young children, whose husband was in the army.

She tried hard to make me welcome but the first evening started badly. I had been given the living room, which had a small table, for my studies, and also for my meals. Dinner was at 6 and I was duly sitting down at the table a few minutes early. The landlady arrived on time with an enamel dish of cottage pie with a nice crisp topping. It looked inviting and exciting to a hungry student. I helped myself and quickly cleared the dish. A few minutes later, the landlady appeared and came to a sudden stop. It then dawned on me that I had consumed the whole family's meal. I never really recovered from my embarrassment and changed 'digs' as soon as an alternative became available.

One other notable student episode was a visit to the Royal Veterinary College in Royal College Street, Camden Town.

The College had been evacuated at the beginning of the war and students had to move from one place to another. Even so, having reached the final year, students were required to attend the small animal clinic in Camden Town for a few weeks. The war was over by the time this rule was established. The four of us who were quite pally, turned up on the Monday morning and attended the first session of the clinic. It so happened that there were two cases, where the advice was that the animal should be 'put down'. This caused the owners – both elderly women – to become distressed. The reaction of the head surgeon at the clinic was so unsympathetic and rude that none of us returned to the clinic and spent the rest of the time sightseeing in the Capital. It was a very poor lesson to graduating students, how not to deal with people losing their pets.

Two vital pieces of education are necessary in practice. Firstly, how to diagnose pain and then, having diagnosed it, deal with whatever surgical or medical treatment was available at the time. Secondly, how to deal with the trauma of suggesting that an animal should be 'put to sleep' and then give the owner support.

These two subjects could only be learnt over time. No lessons were given at College on either topic and one had to learn the hard way through experience. If the visit to the clinic in London was intended to teach us how to deal with these topics, then it failed miserably.

Life in College for the first two years was not all lectures and visits to practices in the holidays. As already mentioned, we were temporarily excused National Service on the understanding that we passed each 'end-of-year' examination. Failure to do so would result in us having to leave our studies and be 'drafted'. In the meantime, however, we had to attend training in the Officer's Training Corps. At the time, this was a tedious necessity, but a thousand times better than being at the front. However, I doubt if we realized it at the time.

* * * * * * * * * * * * * *

The highlight of this 'military' experience came in the Easter holidays in our second year of study. The war was still raging. We were to spend two weeks at a camp on the Blewbury Downs. It was a bitterly cold Easter but, fortunately, the camp consisted of wooden sheds and not tents. Each shed had a coal-burning stove, so we were never cold, once we had turned in for the night.

Half way through the second week, we were informed that, on the Friday before we broke camp, we were to engage the Blewbury Home Guard in a pitched battle on the Downs.

We were shipped by bus to the dropping off point and given instructions. The O.T.C was to occupy a hill and the Home Guard was to attack it and take it, if possible. Each of us was given one blank cartridge and, after using that, we were to shout: "Bang". This would alert the adjudicators that one of the 'enemy' was dead. There were to be adjudicators around the hill and these were supposed to be impartial.

The buses carrying the Home Guard had not yet arrived, so we were lined up for dispersal to our defensive positions.

I was teamed up with another student called Caspari; we were to hide behind some bushes on the high bank beside one of the roads and cause as much disruption as possible to any troops marching up the road.

In the meantime, we had been informed that the battle would commence at 2p.m. with the sound of a long blast on a whistle.

The Officers' Training Corps felt it had the edge [brainwise] over the Blewbury Home Guard, and one of the N.C.O's of the O.T.C. decided that brains were needed to win the battle.

Six of the keenest of our Corps, which did not include me, did not take up their positions on the hillside, but stayed at the dropping off point behind a hedge.

In due course, the buses with the Home Guard arrived, the men disembarked and were lined up in the bus park, put their rifles on the ground and were given their instructions. The chief adjudicator blew his whistle and the battle was under way. However, before the 'enemy' could pick up their rifles and start marching, the six hidden vet students came out from their hiding place and, with rifles cocked, told the Home Guard to surrender 'en bloc'.

All of this was legitimate, as far as we were concerned, but not as far as the chief adjudicator was concerned, who happened to be a member of the Blewbury Home Guard and, in true army fashion, the rules were changed and the six students were dismissed from the exercise as 'dead'.

The battle continued and Caspari and I waited. Soon we heard the marching of feet and a squad appeared round a bend in the road. We then used our two blanks and, hopefully, killed their radio operator and the man carrying the radio equipment. We demonstrated our success to a local adjudicator, who also happened to be a Home Guard man, who declared that we had missed!

We had now declared our position to the 'enemy' and one of them started to crawl through the grass towards us. Caspari let out a couple of "Bangs" which were ignored by the adjudicator and the man kept coming.

Caspari had had enough, he picked up a large lump

of flint, aimed it at the approaching face and let go. His aim was excellent. The flint hit the man where his tin hat met his forehead. The man let out a yell and the adjudicator took our names and we were reported at the end of the battle for not playing fair.

The next day, we were going home and all was forgotten.

The only thing I got from my association with the military was Athletes Crotch, a type of Athletes Foot but in a more sensitive area. Army clothes were never cleaned or disinfected before being handed on to the next user. I decided to treat myself with an application of strong tincture of iodine [much more potent than the ordinary tincture]. The result was a huge blister, which burst within a few days at an inconvenient time. It worked. The infection disappeared together with large areas of skin.

There was still conscription in those days, but if one could get into the Ministry of Agriculture or into a practice that was considered of national importance, then conscription was delayed and subsequently cancelled. I had managed to get the offer of a job as assistant in the practice of Broad and Widden in Lancaster Gate, which specialised in horses. London was still served by 'heavy' horses and carts and these were to remain for several years until lorries started coming off the assembly lines instead of army vehicles. The large 'Shires', 'Clydesdales' and 'Percherons' dominated the streets, but in due course were unable to compete with lorries: lorries did not have to be fed and exercised at weekends.

Failure to exercise horses over the weekend resulted in 'Monday Morning Leg', a swelling of the lower limbs, which meant that the horses needed several days of treatment before they could be put to work again. A horse that could not work was a financial liability, and could not be sustained for too long. The inability to work had to be set against the fact that horse-meat was valuable, and the carcass value of a dead horse, which would be used for human consumption, nearly equalled the purchase price of a replacement. Horse-meat was more palatable than whale meat.

The next five years were to be spent at the Lancaster Gate practice. During that time I learnt a great deal about 'heavy' horses and their ailments and lameness, but with the replacement of the horse-drawn transport of goods by motorised transport, this knowledge became obsolete and I moved on.

In the meantime, however, one had used the student days seeing practice in order to broaden ones knowledge of life in the wider field of veterinary medicine.

THE STAGE

"Remark each anxious toil, each eager strife,
and watch the busy scenes of crowded life"
Samuel Johnson

CHAPTER III

THE NEXT FIVE YEARS

Nine days after graduation found me moving into the premises in Craven Terrace, Lancaster Gate. Craven Terrace is only about one hundred yards long and both sides of the terrace consisted of a continuous row of Victorian red brick houses. At the North end were three or four shops. The street had little character except a feeling of solidity and stability. About three feet in front of each house was an iron railing with an iron gate. The railings had to be retained for obvious safety reasons as they provided against a drop into the basement area below, although many other railings in London had been removed, to be melted down for arms of one sort or another.

The practice house, like all the other houses in the Terrace, was on five floors, basement [or 'area' as it was called], ground floor, first, second and third floors. The basement could be entered by descending steps through the gate in the railings and turning right through a solid brown door into a small hall. A door to the left of the steps was the coal store underneath the pavement; coal was delivered onto the pavement and shovelled through a circular opening in the path, which was covered by a cast iron lid.

The basement was the home of Mr. and Mrs. Major and their daughter Daphne. The Majors were a couple from Cumberland in their mid fifties. Both were gentle people and very reliable. Mrs Major kept the surgeries and waiting rooms clean and looked after me, when the resident Vet, Mr. Widden, was on holiday.

Mr Major answered the door to clients in surgery hours, helped in the dispensary and was always 'on hand' to give assistance. He continually smoked a pipe, and a few years after I joined the practice, he developed cancer of the tongue, which later spread to the throat. Poor Mr. Major died in St Mary's Hospital to everybody's very deep regret. Although mild and somewhat retiring in nature, we found out later that he had received the Military Cross for bravery in the First World War.

Daphne was in her twenties, rather buxom with a very 'English' peaches-and-cream complexion. She worked in the city as a secretary and always seemed cheerful. She later married a soldier, who had been a prisoner of war in Germany for most of the war, and, in due course, moved out into her new home.

The Majors' basement flat occupied most of the lowest floor, but a room at the end of the corridor, from which led the Majors' bedrooms, bathroom and kitchen, was the dispensary.

The dispensary had a bank of mahogany drawers along one side containing medicinal powders. Similar rows of mahogany drawers could be seen in most chemists' shops at the time. These drawers made a grand type of fireplace, as they surrounded an old iron grate. Making up various mixtures of powders was a continuous routine at surgery hours, when dogs and cats were being treated. Individually, most of the powders were innocuous, but, to our surprise, it seemed that, in the right circumstances, they could be explosive. One afternoon, before the two o'clock surgery hour started, Jack, the kennel man, slammed one of the drawers shut and the result was a loud bang and several drawers shot out onto the floor. There must have been some cross contamination of the powders between the drawers, and the friction caused by slamming the drawers produced the ideal situation of the contaminated mixture to produce a violent chemical reaction much like a gunpowder explosion. No person or animal was injured, but the drawers had to be cleaned and fixed back onto the wall.

On the opposite wall was a row of shelves with Winchester bottles full of liquid medicines. Under these shelves were drawers containing various sizes of medicine bottles, together with their appropriate corks. Other drawers contained pillboxes, labels and sundry items of surgical equipment. At the far end of that wall was a rather badly stained china sink with a gas water heater above it. In the centre of the room was a bench under which was a barred kennel for any urgent and emergency case, which needed immediate attention. A gas ring was beside the sink and instruments were sterilized by boiling them in a fish-kettle.

Dispensing medicines was an integral part of veterinary practice.

In those days, there were no pre-packed liquids or tablets, and each client had to wait for medicines to be dispensed. College classes had prepared us for this, as the pharmacology lectures included lessons in preparing liquids and powders. Each powder for small animals had to be wrapped individually and then carefully put in another outer wrapper of white paper and finally into a brown envelope. The Craven Terrace practice was very particular in its presentation of medicines, and each bottle and pillbox would be handed over to the client in a white paper 'outer' and sealed with red sealing wax. Labels would be carefully written with the owner's name and address on it. Pills were bought in bulk from the pharmaceutical supplier and then dispensed when necessary into the round pill boxes. Once a month, the supplier's representative would call to take his order for medicines and try and sell new instruments. He would relate all the local scandal and keep us up-to-date with new medicines and instruments. He was a jovial man from the Pharmaceutical Company Willows, Francis, Butler and Thomson and, from what he said, his territory was the whole of Southern England and the Midlands; he had to travel by public transport due to the continuing fuel shortage.

This meticulous procedure of preparing medicines for small animals did not apply to horse medicines, which were generally dispensed in much larger bottles. Medicine bottle manufacturers did not produce larger bottles than 12 fluid ounces. The liquid horse medicines or 'drenches', as they were commonly called, were dispensed in discarded beer or wine bottles and advantage was taken of the differently shaped bottles that were readily available. Jack would visit the local waste dump and collect the bottles when required

For convenience, these drenches were given simple names to make it easy for the horse keepers to identify. The major stables would have a stock of bottles of each drench. Night calls could be reduced by telling the horse-keeper to give the sick animal a particular 'drench', and he would know immediately what medicine to administer.

'NUMBER ONE' drench was a saturated solution of Epsom Salts in a Guinness bottle. Used as a mild laxative.

'NUMBER TWO' drench was a mixture of Parish's Food

and quinine in a hock bottle. Used as a tonic.

'DIRTY WHITE' drench was a mixture of kaolin and morphine in a claret bottle. Used for mild colic

'EMBROCATION' was, as its name implies, a bottle of homemade embrocation, used for sprains and strains and was dispensed in a Gordon's Gin bottle.

Marmalade jars would contain a soothing mixture made up of molasses and bran. This was to be given to horses after they had been subjected to having their teeth rasped. Horses' teeth are very large and often develop rough edges; these irritate the inside of the mouth, resulting in the fact that the animal finds it too painful to eat. This bran and molasses mixture would help soothe the sore mouth after rasping away the rough edges.

A daybook was kept in the dispensary and filled in with details of the owner's name, animal's name, diagnosis and medicine prescribed, together with the fee charged. The larger fees were always invoiced in guineas [£1.05]. Regular clients were sent invoices every quarter and, rather unexpectedly, there were few 'bad' debts.

Jack would make the horse drenches up in his spare time and the car would always have a stock of each drench in the boot.

At the far end of the dispensary was a door leading out to a small yard, which separated the main house from the mews house at the back. This yard was used quite frequently by those dogs, which had been given an enema after treatment for tapeworms. Jack, the kennel-man, had the unenviable task to examine the result of the enema and report back whether the head of the tapeworm could be found.

The main house was the last house in the terrace, not by any architectural design, but because Hitler had landed a bomb nearby and left a large area of desolation next to the house. This bombed area stretched back to the Church at the end of Sussex Gardens and across the road to another large area of desolation. These flattened areas were covered with dust and rubble, which had not been removed and were highlighted by weeds, struggling, like the human population, to survive the war.

The ground floor consisted of a consulting room, a large waiting room, a large office and a small anti-room. Every door, window frame and skirting board was painted 'Builders Brown' and this added an air of sadness to the whole building. The walls were covered with embossed wallpaper, which had been 'refreshed' at infrequent intervals with cream paint. It would seem that the last rejuvenation was years old, as the cream paint had soured to a murky greyish brown. The floor was covered with 'lino', equally past its useful date and was again a muddy colour with worn patches revealing the dirty floorboards underneath. This picture of desolation and deprivation was not abnormal, after five years of war. No client entering the practice would expect freshly painted and hygienic rooms, each would have his or her mind fixed on where the next meal was coming from and how much the treatment was likely to cost and if it could be afforded.

The first floor was occupied by a **Mrs. Matthews** and her daughter. They were lessees and had very little contact with members of the practice and gave the impression that they had 'seen better times'. The daughter worked as secretary to a Member of Parliament. She was a good tennis player, or so she told us. The Matthews' actions gave the impression that they were ashamed of having to live in a flat, associated with a veterinary practice, with its smells and noise.

Mr. and Mrs. Widden and their baby son had their bedrooms on the second floor, together with a large drawing room and a large kitchen, where we had our meals. Mr Widden was the resident vet and was in the process of taking over the practice from Mr Broad at the time I joined the practice.

I had a room on the top floor. There was also the communal bathroom and a spare room. The only time I saw the spare room used was to 'lay out' Mrs Widden's mother, when she died; I was asked to pay my respects and saw a dead body for the first time in my life, although death was a daily occurring experience to many Londoners from Hitler's bombing.

My room was quite large, got hot in the summer and overlooked a pub, 'The Mitre', on the opposite side of Craven Terrace. Saturday evenings saw the start of an invasion of Irish drinkers and, at closing time, I was invariably kept awake by choruses of 'Danny Boy' and 'Have you ever been across the sea to Ireland'. Unfortunately, it seemed that the singers never went across the sea to Ireland and instead stayed to keep me awake. Fortunately, however, the opening hours were not very long and, at about 11 o'clock, the crowds, which stayed to sing away their troubles, soon dispersed and went home. Occasionally, there were times when music gave way to aggression and there were threats of fights, but from my high room, I never saw a real fight. Mostly, the fighters depended on their friends to hold them back and restrain them, which seemed to be an essential part of the ritual.

Across the yard from the dispensary was the mews house: a two-story building with ground floor facilities for boarding and hospital cases. These kennels occupied the first half of the ground floor. Behind them was a garage for two cars.

The first floor of the mews was a small flat occupied by the kennel man Jack and his wife Joan. This flat had only recently been rebuilt, as it had suffered structural damage by the bomb.

The kennel area, where animals were boarded, and where post-surgical and medical cases were hospitalised, had an operating table in the middle and, when operations were in progress, the surrounding boarders seemed to have a great time as spectators. One was under the impression that the animals relished witnessing operations, that relieved their boredom. The kennels were always full and generally consisted of cats and dogs, in equal proportions. Only rarely did one see an exotic animal, but we did have a monkey staying there for some weeks. This was not a patient, but it stayed with us because its owner had to go into hospital for an operation. The monkey in question suffered from a chronic scaly skin infection, which, according to the owner, had failed to respond to treatment from other vets. The owner provided the food, which, I think, was a mixture of dried vegetables and fresh fruit. The monkey was interested in everything that was going on in the kennels and would stretch its arm through the bars of its kennel to any passer-by. It had the habit of reaching out and grabbing a handful of dog's meat when Jack was feeding the other animals and Jack was the first to notice that the skin condition was improving rapidly; and we assumed that the meat it was stealing must have provided some nutrient that it had been deprived of in its vegetable diet. We decided that, in its natural habitat, the leaves it ate would have insects or caterpillars on them and that these would be providing the necessary proteins or vitamins.

Exotic animals had not made their way into the human world of keeping pets, mainly because they were not readily available from pet shops. The odd snake was presented to us for treatment and, if it was for the removal of external parasites, then we undertook routine treatment, but other conditions were sent up the road to the Zoo in Regent's Park, where experts were only too willing to help.

Children would bring in wild animals or birds, which they had found in the Kensington Gardens nearby: hedgehogs, which had been mauled by cats or dogs, and the occasional frogs, newts and toads.

* * * * * * * * * * * * * *

If we examine the old creation myths of Genesis, tradition tells that, since the serpent [snake] was the first creature mentioned, it is therefore accepted as the first creature to be created. The question has been raised as to whether the snake was there before God created the world. Nevertheless, it was the snake that tempted Eve, and the downfall of mankind resulted.

A story was told in the Middle Ages that the toad saved the world at the time of the second creation where God, having grown tired of mankind's sins, decided to 'blot out' the world.

He relented and, because Noah had been a 'good man', gave us all a second chance. The flood enabled a new world without the Devil, or so He thought. The Bible mentions Noah and his sons, but without mentioning Noah's wife. This enabled the ecclesiastical writers of the medieval 'Mystery Plays' to highlight their misogynistic attitude, with the result that Noah's wife became the first 'shrew' of Christendom.

The story goes that Noah's wife took umbrage that she had not been told why Noah was building the Ark. The Devil got wind of the recreation of the human race and sought the help of Noah's wife, and between them, they concocted a brew which, when given to Noah, caused him to confess all that God had promised. Despite the Devil's and Noah's wife's attempt to prevent the Ark being built, it was built in time and completed with the help of an angel. With the aid of Noah's wife, the Devil also entered the Ark, with the intention of drowning the human race. The Devil caused havoc, which included the rejection of abstinence. Things were going badly for the Noah household until, one day, Noah discovered that the Devil was on board with him. The Devil was cursed by Noah, to such an extent, that he gnawed a hole in the Ark and escaped. A toad filled the hole and enabled the new creation to occur.

It was not long before the Devil struck again and mankind, in the form of Noah, sinned again by drinking alcohol and getting drunk soon after reaching dry land.

The Devil was free again, mankind was lost again and the woman was blamed again.

* * * * * * * * * * * * * *

In the kennel area was a large wooden chest for storing biscuit meal, and a metal container for raw meat. Of course, there were no refrigerators, so the building had a mixed aroma of dogs, cats, biscuits and slightly rotten meat. All of this provided an ideal environment for cockroaches; these could never be eradicated and were accepted as part of the environment. I never heard that they invaded Jack's upstairs flat, but assumed that their living was so good downstairs that they had no need to venture any further afield. In the daytime, the cockroaches were out of sight, but at night they emerged in their thousands. This left two choices when having to get the car out for night visits: either turning on the lights and seeing a floor covered with cockroaches, all swiftly heading for shelter from the sudden illumination or, alternatively, walking through the kennels in the dark and crunching over the insects with every footfall. Neither was very enjoyable.

On occasions, the kennels were also safe havens for both sides of the law. Next to the mews cottage at the back was a small public house. Here, most business was done in the lunch hours and the early afternoon. The drinkers were of a rougher kind than those in the pub opposite my bedroom. Fights were not uncommon and there was no protective ritual. Those were the days when policemen were on foot and there was always a local 'bobby' to protect the public. The local 'bobby' was a friendly type and not too keen on getting embroiled in physical violence. It was not unusual to meet him in the kennels when there was a fight in the mews outside. He would sneak into the kennels when trouble was beginning, and Jack would keep a lookout and tell the policeman when the trouble had subsided and then the guardian of the law would appear only when the fight was over. He would resume his beat when it was safe to do so.

In a similar fashion, a certain criminal would sneak into the kennels for safety from arrest.

Betting on horses was not a controlled affair, as it is now. The bookies would rely on 'runners', who took bets from punters in the pub and 'run' to the bookmakers in Praed Street, taking the bets on slips of paper. The local 'runner' would let himself into the kennels for refuge, as soon as he was told that the law was about. Once again, in true Cockney fashion, Jack would tip him off when the police had moved on, and the runner would go about his business. I can recall only one occasion when the 'bobby' and the 'runner' were in the kennels at the same time and both lit a cigarette and chatted, parting in due course as good friends, each knowing that life in post-war England was not a time for personal confrontation. We had all had our fill of fighting.

The practice was predominantly a heavy horse practice. I had been there as a student and knew the ins and outs of it. Fortunately, the training at the Veterinary College was geared to horses. The anatomy of the horse dominated the third year and the horse was the animal to be dissected.

At the beginning of the third year, a horse would be destroyed, immediately pumped full of formalin solution and then suspended in a stall in one of the college outbuildings. Each student would be given a part of the horse to be dissected under the supervision of the anatomy lecturer. The smell of formalin was everywhere and it permeated ones clothing, hair and skin. It probably permeated the lungs as well, but 'health and safety' regulations and legislation were years away.

Surgery and medicine tutorials at college were based on equine problems and the medicine part of the course seemed to be dominated by lectures on colic, strangles and all kinds of problems related to strained limbs.

All of this gave a good basic knowledge for going into a horse practice. The main practice income relied on contractual work with the big concerns, where horses were vital for distribution. The main railways, GWR, LMS, LNER and SR, had their own stables and their own veterinary surgeons. We dealt with the large coal companies, such as 'Rickett Cockerell', 'Charrington Warren' and 'Wally Spiers', together with the various breweries, bakeries and any other horse user throughout London. The contracts with the coal companies were on a 'per capita' basis. The practice received two shillings and sixpence [twelve and a half new pence] per horse per quarter and, for that, it had to provide all treatment and visits free of any further charge.

The London carthorse was a delightful animal, docile, unflappable and sometimes very stubborn, but in a friendly way. Lameness was a continuing and increasing problem, as the wood block streets were gradually being replaced with unyielding tarmac metalled roads. The wood blocks and cobblestones gave a surface, on which the hooves could grip, whereas the new smooth roads resulted in more problems with an increase in damaged knees and sprains.

The diagnosis of lameness depends on two factors. One is a good knowledge of the anatomy of the horse's legs and the other is the experience of the Veterinary Surgeon.

The initial problem was to decide which leg was the lame one, and here the horseman was on his own ground and would wait for the young graduate, like me, to make mistakes. The answer to this problem was to ask the horseman which was the bad leg, before you even saw the horse or, if that was not possible, to ask him to pick up the bad leg to let you look at its shoe and hoof. If even that was not possible, then you were on your own. Many of these causes of lameness could be relieved by corrective shoeing, and this meant that the practice had to have its own shoeing facilities with its own smiths, fires and anvils.

Craven Terrace was no place for shoeing, although it was not uncommon to be called out of the front door and find a coster's pony tied to the front railings waiting to be examined. These smaller ponies were sprightlier than the heavies, but still no problem to handle. Generally, they were well groomed and well fed; there was a fondness and empathy between horse and coster. This empathy was derived from the respect for the pony for its loyalty and the fact that the animal was the essential breadwinner. It was often said that the costermonger would prefer to spend the night tending his sick pony than being with his wife. On the rare occasions that one met the wife, this was quite understandable. Even three or four ponies queuing up to be attended to, all tied to the railings, caused neither surprise nor resentment to the local population.

STAR STREET

The heart of the horse practice was at the other end of Praed Street, about a mile from the Craven Terrace premises. It was situated in **Star Street**, a small street, leading straight on to The Edgware Road. It was a run-down street about 50 yards long with old decrepit dark red-bricked rows of disjointed buildings. Painted on the end wall of one of these buildings was a faded name 'BROAD', about 6 feet high, and underneath 'VETERINARY SURGEON'.

In the 1940's, The Royal College was strict as to how Veterinary surgeons advertised their premises. The name could only be a few inches high on a brass plate of defined size. I could never understand how Old Man Broad, got away with his name in very large letters. It was more common in those days to get a reprimand from The Royal College for an oversized nameplate than for negligence.

The downtrodden building in Star Street was two stories high. At the ground level, there was a small window on the left side. The rest of the front of the building was a large double size garage-type door with a smaller door, set into the large door, to give access for people to enter. The large door was opened each morning by the chief farrier, who lived in a small flat on the ground floor. Behind the large door were the three 'fires', each with its own bellows and anvil. Two other farriers lived nearby and would arrive at 7.30 sharp to get their fires going and wait for the first horses to arrive. By eight o'clock, the place was hot, noisy and smelly. There was no ventilation in the farriery and, by nine o'clock, the building was full of smoke from the fires and from the burning hooves. Routine shoeing was no problem but, where lameness was involved, each shoe had to be tailor-made to try and correct the deformity in the hoof or to raise the heel or toe to ease the pain.

Sometimes, in the winter, to enter Star Street was like entering the biblical picture of Hell. Smoke, red-hot fires, hammering, all gave a picture of demonic activity, and the smell of burning keratin from the hooves added to the picture of Hades.

At the far end of the building was an area set out as dog kennels for longer-term boarders. Twice a day, Jack would cycle or get a lift from Craven Terrace to Star Street, to feed the boarders. There was a small anteroom, where the practice took in dogs, suffering from distemper, and I believe that it was the only practice to have a distemper hospital. Needless to say, very few dogs – if any – survived a long stay in the hospital. It was a time before efficient distemper vaccines were available, and if the poor dog was admitted on a wrong diagnosis, it very soon developed the disease and died.

Nevertheless, Star Street provided me with years of happiness. One of the long-term boarders was a lovely Corgi bitch, which had been left for some months by its female owner and was everybody's favourite. The owner was a wealthy middle-aged woman who, in my opinion, bought the dog originally as an accessory to one of her 'going-out' outfits. Fashion had changed and the colour of the corgi did not match the new season's colours. Miniature poodles were the 'in fashion' breed as they could be adorned with accessories and trimmed to add to the owner's image. In the end, I contacted the owner, who had continued to pay the boarding fees on time, and offered to buy the dog from her. We agreed a price of £10, which was nearly a week's wages. I named her Mopsy and, during the course of her life, she gave endless enjoyment to me, my wife and later my children.

Star Street was certainly Dickensian in character and was doomed to extinction as horses became less and less necessary for the growing commercial post-war London. By the time I left the practice some years later, Star Street was closed for shoeing and only the boarding kennels remained. To compensate, Craven Terrace was thriving under the diligent care of Mr. Widden, who had forecast the demise of the 'horse practice' and had developed a reputation for being a small animal expert.

The various people in the practice formed a 'small-knit' community, which had its own interdependent structure.

THE ACTORS

"Whence are we, and why are we?
Of what scene. The actors or spectators?"
Shelley

CHAPTER IV

THE ACTORS

In retrospect, the practice became a stage with a close-knit cast of actors. **Mr Stanley Broad**, 'The Old Man' was the originator and had spent decades working there. When I joined, he was on the verge of retiring and lived with his second wife away from the practice, in Farnham. This meant that he would arrive at Paddington Station around mid-morning, do the necessary rounds and return after tea. The journey to Paddington Station required him to cut through the passage by the church and then walk along Sussex Gardens.

Sussex Gardens was notorious, in the forties as a stamping ground for prostitutes. They could be seen most evenings wandering up and down looking for men and, if they spotted a likely one, would walk up to them, quickly confront them, open their coats to reveal 'the goods' and say; "Hello darling".

On one particular occasion, Mr Widden was driving along Sussex Gardens on the way to visit a client and saw 'The Old Man' heading for the station and twice being accosted in the conventional manner. To the 'Hello darling', he raised his 'Antony Eden' hat and walked on.

The next morning, Mr Widden mentioned what he had seen and asked 'The Old Man' if he knew who the ladies were.

"No", said 'The Old Man', I thought they were maybe clients of ours".

"No", replied Mr Widden, "I thought you were possibly a client of theirs".

'The Old Man' did little work with any animal other the horse. To him, cats and dogs were unimportant and, in the early days of the practice these would be passed on and seen by Jack. He would realize that the horse income would decrease in a few years, but by then, he would have retired. He was a big man, not fat but big-boned. He had a florid complexion with a purple, pitted nose. The nose, to those who did not know him, would have been from heavy drinking, but, in fact, he was not a heavy drinker.

He always wore a dark suit with a white shirt and a bow tie and a winged collar. When visiting the stables, he wore a long serge overcoat and his usual 'Anthony Eden' hat; he presented an imposing figure to all who met him.

He was somewhat deaf and, when not in communication with someone, would hum away to himself. On one occasion, when working with his back to us and humming away, Jack said to me in a soft voice, and for a bit of fun, "What is the tune that the old man is humming?"

Before I could answer 'The Old Man' turned round and retorted: "Mind your own bloody business!"

Jack was unperturbed and walked off and we all wondered just how deaf 'The Old Man' really was.

His imposing manner and his size – he was about six foot two – resulted in most clients, whether rich or poor, commoner or aristocrat, being overawed.

His years in practice in central London, near affluent areas like Mayfair and Chelsea, had alerted him to the idiosyncrasies of city life away from the working class cockney horse keepers. His response was a tendency to generalise. He warned me, in the first week that I was there, to beware of people with 'titles', as they did not expect to pay. I should always try and get cash 'on the spot'. I think this prejudice was partly based on his contempt for them as pet owners, which to him meant tedious and spoilt cats and dogs.

It was not uncommon for him to put the brokers in to collect bad debts, particularly from the aristocracy, and I think he rather enjoyed it.

I can recall a 'phone call from Lady X to the practice; she was in a panic saying that there were two men in her hall demanding payment and asking what she should do. She got a curt reply: "Pay them madam!"

Were meanness and aloofness in-bred characteristics of the aristocracy in those days?

Lord F. arrived one day to collect his wife's poodle, which had been trimmed by Jack. Jack, himself, took the animal upstairs on its lead expecting his usual tip, bent down to pick up the dog to hand it over and was met by a stern command.

"Don't touch him, I don't know where your hands have been!"

Jack did not reply and his Lordship failed to give him his tip. In fact, his Lordship showed his superiority by wiping his feet on the way out!

There were, however, exceptions to this rule and, after a few years in the practice, I was able to discard some of the bigotry of 'The Old Man'.

The Duchess of G was a very nice and charming old lady. She was nearly blind and had a Pekingese, which was equally nearly blind. The result was that it kept knocking its head on furniture and, as a result, developed chronic ulcerated eyes. At that time there was little effective remedy, for ulcerated eyes and the treatment prescribed by Mr Widden was the drastic application of a silver nitrate stick to cauterise the ulcer.

Visiting her in her flat in Mount Street was always a pleasure and tea would always be waiting for me.

The flat was expensively furnished and the carpets were of a very fine quality. What the Duchess did not realize was that the Peke frequently cocked his leg up against the legs of the furniture, which resulted in corroded patches of carpet around each leg of chairs, tables and settees. The Duchess was oblivious to this and would have accepted it, even if she had been aware of the damage that was being done. The Peke was the apple of her eye.

One visit provided an insight into the attitude of my opposite number in the medical profession. I arrived one morning, climbed the steps to the front door and found another visitor waiting to be let in.

He was in a smart suit and was carrying a bag similar to mine. I was in my usual ex-RAF blue shirt. I got a sour look from him and noticed that he had a large bunch of hair on each cheek under the eyes. That alerted me to the fact that he was slightly 'off key'.

He glared at me and asked in a disdainful tone of voice:
"Are you the Vet?"
"Yes", I said, "Are you the Doctor?"
"Yes", he said, "I hope mine dies before yours".
I let him see his patient first.

I bet he didn't get cakes and sandwiches for tea – if he did, I hoped my patient cocked his leg up against his medical bag.

The 'Old Man' would never visit small animal clients in their homes; he left that to Mr Widden and me. His life was in his horses and visiting them gave him all the satisfaction that he needed.

I always felt that it was a backward move when the profession, for financial reasons, limited home visits to a minimum, for not only did it break the monotony of continuous surgeries, but it also gave an insight into how people lived and, on occasions, even helped in the diagnosis of the patient's ailment.

One example occurred when a nervous dog came into the surgery, there was the immediate problem of trying to discover the reason for this anxiety.

I had been treating this Peke, which seemed unduly frightened of making any move. Sedatives were of no real help except to make the dog sleepy. By good fortune, I was asked to pay a visit to the house, due to the owner's illness. It was a nice house, well furnished and clean. The owner was a quiet woman who was obviously very fond of her pet. The piece of furniture that I didn't expect to see was a parrot's cage, housing a brightly coloured bird, which greeted me with a squawk. I made a quick mental note not to take too much notice of it, as I might have found myself being asked to clip its nails; cutting a parrot's nails always resulted in a squabble between me and the parrot, with the parrot generally turning out to be the winner. The Peke had kept a low profile in the hall, but reluctantly responded to its owner's "Come here".

The dog slowly entered the room to be met with a sharp cry of, "Sit down".

The dog sat down.

The owner seemed slightly amused and went to pacify the poor animal.

The command to 'Sit down' had not come from the owner, however, but from the parrot. I was told that this command was the only phrase that the parrot could utter, but it had shattered the poor dog's nerve. All I could do, other than keeping the two animals away from each other or getting rid of one, was to suggest some form of separation. No doubt, the modern 'Animal Behaviourist' would have a more positive solution; probably by teaching the parrot to say: "Good boy".

A similar episode involved two different species but, like

the Peke and the parrot, a home visit gave the answer to the problem.

This time, it was a cat that was suffering from a nervous disposition and was showing symptoms of starvation and a bizarre habit of looking over its shoulder all of the time. A home visit gave the answer. Besides the cat, the client owned two small monkeys. These were running, or more accurately, climbing all over the room, mainly shooting up the curtains and settling on the curtain rail. At frequent intervals, one of them would leap onto the cat's back, hold on tightly and enjoy the ride like a jockey on a horse, until it got fed up with the cat's acrobatics and let go and climbed up the curtain again. The cat, no matter how quick its reactions, never seemed to be able to scratch or bite the monkey, which may have partly solved the problem. Instead all the poor cat could do was to live a life of forever looking over its shoulder to try and avoid the next attack. Again, separation was the only answer and I never saw the end of this particular case.

Home visits did have other rewards than merely seeing the environment in which the animal lived; it gave an insight into the life-style of the owner.

A late night call to a flat in Kilburn found me in a room with four men playing cards at a round table. The centre light of the room was suspended low over the green baize covering; the men were in shirt sleeves with arm bands holding up their cuffs from the surface of the table and two players had green eye shades. They were playing poker and the picture was reminiscent of similar gambling scenes with George Raft and Humphry Bogart on the cinema screen.

It was not the scene, however, that interested me, it was the face of one of the players. I recalled that he had been a 'bad debt' three years previously, who had disappeared from the scene and could not be traced. I had no qualms about tackling him on his overdue payment, mainly because it was ten o'clock at night and all I had been called out for was to cut an Alsation's nails. He reluctantly paid mainly so as not to lose face with his accomplices. I discovered later, on recounting the story to another client, that it was not uncommon for three or four people to rotate their residences every year or so to avoid paying bills and that every three or four years, depending on how many people were in the intrigue, they would end up again in their original flat.

In the forties, it was not uncommon to send out accounts every quarter; the population was more stable than now and property was in short supply in London, where so many houses had been destroyed in the bombing. But, the practice was near a main line railway station and that meant that there was always a number of people with a nomadic disposition. One just had to assess those clients who were reliable citizens and those 'chancers' who would skip payment if they possibly could.

Another night call, this time to visit a flat just off the Edgware Road, gave me a further insight into a different aspect of human life.

I was greeted, at the door, by a blond woman in her early thirties. She was only partly dressed and very agreeable and led me into a rather sumptuous sitting room, in which were three or four more women of similar ages. These were also in various stages of undress and 'make up'. All greeted me in a friendly way and were interested in how I was treating a rather superficial wound on the leg of their poodle.

They all thanked me as I was leaving, and I was paid cash and left. Going through the daybook the next day, Mr. Widden queried me on the visit; I told him what I had done and that cash had been paid. He and Jack, who were in the room, smiled and I was informed that I had visited a brothel. Being close to Sussex Gardens meant that it was not infrequent to be visited by prostitutes or to visit them in their flats. Many of them kept pets, and, without exception, they were friendly, appreciative and always paid cash.

Despite his stern exterior, 'The Old Man' did have his sense of humour though. The telephone system in those days depended on calls being dealt with manually from the exchange and wrong numbers were common. Answering wrong numbers gave him an opportunity to show his wit. Whenever he got a wrong number, he would announce that he was either

'The Battersea Bad Egg Company' or 'Underwater Acrobats'. Little did he realize that the latter would be part of the Olympic Games in fifty years or so. Nevertheless, he had some personal satisfaction in demonstrating his sense of humour and he really thought these replies were the ultimate amusing responses.

He never really got the hang of the modern world. Towards the end of his time in the practice, more cars and lorries were on the roads; roundabouts were being introduced onto the busy road junctions and traffic lights were being installed in greater numbers.

To him, roundabouts were an unnecessary evil and very often, when I used to drive him around London from stable to stable, he would order me to go round a roundabout the wrong way, when there was little traffic about. He considered that traffic lights were only of value, when other traffic was approaching from the left or right. At other times, he would get quite frustrated when I stopped for the lights to change, when there was no visible traffic likely to cause an accident

"Go on", he would say, "there's nothing coming".

I had to satisfy the boss and keep within the law. There were times when I was too nervous to disobey 'The Old Man', and I broke the law, but luckily, I never got caught.

I acted as chauffeur, because he had difficulty driving cars. To him, double de-clutching was an enigma; he could not co-ordinate the gear lever with putting his foot on the clutch. When he did drive, we knew he was approaching by the grating of his gears, and Jack was convinced that he could hear the tune of "The Blue Bells of Scotland" on the gearbox.

I got to know London very well and it was not uncommon for the two of us to leave Star Street at 11a.m. and then visit stables in King's Cross, Alexandra Palace, Petticoat Lane, Crystal Palace, Kew Gardens, Shepherd's Bush and be back at Craven Terrace for lunch at 1 o'clock.

* * * * * * * * * * * * *

Mr Widden was a different person; he had seen the light, not in a religious way, but in a veterinary way. He saw the 'horse practice' diminishing and he moved towards making it a 'small animal' practice. He had his idiosyncrasies; he spent his evenings doing petit-point for his dining room chairs, whilst I was expected to play Bezique with Mrs. Widden.

In due course, he became an expert at delivering Pekingese puppies by using forceps.

The Pekingese became a very popular pet in Central London and Mayfair, and many women decided that extra cash could be made by breeding them. The puppies had large heads and whelping was difficult. Over a relatively short period of time, his fame spread throughout the Pekingese breeders' community and the breeders would come from all over London and further afield. On one particular occasion, he flew to India to be present at the whelping of one of the Maharaja's pets, for which he got £300 plus a gold cigarette case and a carved cedar-wood chest. He was a good Veterinary Surgeon and deserved his fame – I was never able to equal his skill and most Pekingese breeders would not see me, even for the most mundane procedure.

The Widdens rarely went out in the evenings and seemed to prefer staying in and listening to the wireless. Both had an interest in classical music, but never went to concerts, although they were so close to the Albert Hall and Wigmore Hall.

Mr Widden painted in watercolour and tried each year to get a painting into the Summer Exhibition at the Royal Academy, but never succeeded. His artistic talent did, however, have a bizarre twist to it, as he had the ceiling of his large lounge papered in brown wrapping paper, on which he stuck cut-out stars, a moon and the sun with its rays shining across the heavens. I never dared to ask him what this meant to him.

Funnily enough, after being in the practice and 'living in' for over five years I never got to calling him by his Christian name – it was always – 'Mr Widden'. Even to this day, I cannot recall what his Christian name was.

At one time I got an eye infection from one of the animals and had to go into hospital. There, I fell in love with a nurse and later married her. There was no chance of getting Mrs. Matthews out of her flat so I had to move on and find an assistantship with living accommodation.

* * * * * * * * * * * * * *

Jack, the kennel man, was a typical Cockney and full of fun. He was about forty years old when I joined the practice. He was small with a round boyish face, pale complexion, large forehead with black hair smoothed down with Brylcream. He always reminded me of Stanley Lupino, a Music Hall character of the day, who would not be remembered now by the younger generations.

Jack would handle and immobilise the dogs and cats whilst we examined them and, for extra cash, would trim the Poodles, Scotties, Westies, Terriers, Spaniels and any mongrel that needed a long shaggy coat trimmed for the summer months.

The rear mews house, in Brook Mews, had been affected by the bomb, which had flattened most of Brook Street and, although the kennel area was sound, the flat above it needed a lot of rebuilding. It was only when the rebuilding had been completed that Jack got married and was able to move in. It was at a time, when I was 'seeing practice', that the wedding took place but, being in war-time, it had to be a modest affair. Even so, Jack wore a dark suit and Jane a light blue two-piece.

The ceremony was in the Registry Office on the Marylebone Road; there seemed to be few relatives to cheer the happy couple and neither Jack nor Jane ever mentioned their past, except that Jane, at some time, had been a chorus girl and later worked in a munitions factory. I never knew how Jack had avoided conscription, but in those days, one never asked questions – probably a hang-over from the war-time brain-washing that 'careless talk costs lives'.

The honeymoon was two nights in Brighton, but this was preceded by a visit to Highbury to see the Arsenal play Tottenham Hotspur. Jack and Jane took a bottle of whisky with them, which was probably one of the wedding presents. From the match they took a train to Brighton and a taxi to the small 'Bed and Breakfast' house, which had been previously booked.

From here, Jack takes up the tale as follows.

They booked in and had a fish and chip supper in one

of the cafes on the front and went to their bedroom – a few hours elapsed and, in the middle of the night, Jane decided she wanted to 'spend a penny'. The W.C. was up the corridor ['en-suites' had not been invented then]. Jane did not want to venture in her 'nightie' up the dark corridor, so Jack, in his inventive Cockney way, suggested that he took the aspidistra out of its brass container – the plant itself was in an earthen ware flower pot – and Jane could use the decorated brass container. Early the next morning, Jack intended to sneak out with the container and tip the contents down the lavatory pan. This ploy was only partially successful. The brass container had a serrated rim and poor Jane was left with a 'scored' bottom, which she claimed, lasted for days. Whether this interfered with their nuptials was never mentioned.

However, the trip up the corridor was avoided; Jack had left the plant on the floor and put the brass holder back onto the dressing table. It would seem that it was a warm night, for the widow was left open. During the night, one of the curtains was blown into the container and, by the process of absorption and osmosis or some such physical phenomenon, the urine was siphoned up the curtain, which left it a soaking mass of chintz. Both Jack and Jane were horrified when they saw what had happened; they had a quick breakfast, made their excuses, and left as soon as they had paid and before the landlady or chambermaid had a chance to make up the room. This honeymoon really ended up as a wet rag.

Jack was not really a 'horse man' and his only real contact with the main part of the practice was to chat with the costermongers, who, early in the morning, would bring their ponies to the front door for attention . He was, however, very good with dogs and cats and came into his own, when the small animal side of the business began to expand.

He had developed a kind of canine half-nelson neck-hold, which he could put, in a flash, on any dog. The patient would be immediately immobilised and ready for examination by one of the vets. In the course of time, he became good at anaesthetising cats. The technique was simple; he would grab the cat by the scruff of the neck, thus avoid being bitten or scratched, and then hold it forcibly face down on an army blanket on the operating table.

All that the cat was able to do with its claws was to dig them into the blanket and no harm was done.

The anaesthetic was a mixture of chloroform and ether on a pad of cotton wool. The anaesthetic 'machine' was a large empty jam jar, into which the pad of anaesthetic was placed and the cat's head then plunged in as far as it would go. After an initial struggle, the animal fell asleep. Recovery was rapid after the operation and there were no obvious side effects. Jack always claimed his death rate was no worse than in later years, when more up-to-date anaesthetics and anaesthetic machines were used.

Jack was a key element in the practice, when it came to the three essential aspects in any animal's life: birth, marriage and death.

The two most popular breeds of dogs in the post-war years were cocker spaniels and Pekingese. Cocker spaniels were being bred in large numbers in order to satisfy demand and were getting more and more bad tempered as interbreeding concentrated all the unwanted traits of the breed. Pekingese were not so easy to breed and many puppies were born dead, due to whelping problems.

Although Jack was never allowed to use forceps, when whelping problems occurred, he was expert at tending the bitches and gave them all the care that was possible, showing the mother each puppy as it was born. Before that, he would have carefully dried the puppy and cleared the mucous from its mouth. Pekingese, because of their facial structure, were bad breathers.

Mating dogs was Jack's speciality. He claimed he could mate any dog with any bitch that he was presented with. The bitch would be placed on the grooming table with her lead attached to an upright piece of mechanics that Jack had invented. This was at the head of the table, so that she was unable to turn round and bite either Jack or the dog. The dog would be lifted onto the table behind her and Jack would get to work. He would keep the animals in for a whole day, so time was not at a premium, and Jack showed endless patience in his manipulations of the often incompatible couple. At the end of a successful day, he was allowed to take the dog and the bitch up to their respective owners and collect his tips.

Owners, out of some false sense of natural justice, always felt that it was the kind thing to do to let a dog mate a bitch once in its life and also to let a bitch be mated once in hers. I often wondered if this reflected the client's own courtship philosophy.

One such mating incidence, however, ended in a satisfied dog and a satisfied bitch and an insulted owner.

Hannibal was a very large bulldog owned by the wife of the proprietor of one of the best hotels in Eastbourne. He was a very nice and gentle dog, who was a frequent visitor to the surgery for attention to his eyes. He would come up to Craven Terrace with his owner in their chauffeur-driven Rolls. Against our advice, Hannibal was to have his one big sexual outing and a bulldog bitch was selected from the ads. in 'OUR DOGS'. Both arrived in the morning, but the owners did not know each other. The bitch was very young and small, but Jack succeeded to get them mated after several hours of trying. The bitch's owner arrived first and was just leading her bulldog out of the front door (both owner and bitch looked happy), when Hannibal's owner arrived. She noted the smallness of the bitch.

After a short time, Jack brought Hannibal into the waiting-room (both Jack and Hannibal looked happy). Jack, because he had just pocketed a large tip from the bitch's owner. Hannibal because of his new experience and, if dogs can project their thoughts forward, was gleefully anticipating his next trip up to town.

Jack always got on well with 'The Eastbourne Duchess', as we named her, but never in the past had their chatter related to anything more than trivial time-passing gossip. To Jack, this meeting was no different from any other and mating canines was all part of his day's work. To Hannibal's owner, this was a special day, and she had spent most of it in Regent Street and Bond Street, worrying about her Hannibal's progress.

She patted Hannibal and asked Jack if the bulldog bitch, she had just seen leaving, was Hannibal's 'wife'.

"She's the one", said Jack, " a very friendly little bitch".

"But", said the Duchess, "she's so small, are you sure they were mated?".

Jack sensed some concern in her voice and felt his expertise was in question.

He came out with one of his favourite and reassuring expressions.

"Madam", he said, " Don't worry, it'll stretch a mile before it'll tear an inch".

The Duchess went pale, because she knew what he meant but had never had it explained so specifically before.

She had a quiet word with Mr. Widden on the 'phone the next day in a mild protest. We felt that, in order to legitimize the event and so feel free to discuss the conversation openly with her friends, she found it necessary to retain her reputation in the outside world by putting in a complaint. We were all sure it would be the talking point in the Eastbourne ladies' bridge sessions for days to come.

Jack was not reprimanded, as we all felt that he had dealt with a delicate anatomical problem in a very positive manner.

As to deaths, Jack's adroitness with the Prussic Acid bottle – the recognised way of destroying animals – was accepted by the Vets, as he had more experience in this than any other member of the practice.

Leaving college as a graduate and going straight into a practice was a daunting experience, but less so in the nineteen forties than in the twenty first century. In the immediate post-war era, the graduate was required to 'see practice' in the holidays and there he would have had the opportunity of working on his own and thus gaining valuable experience. Even so, the new assistant would need time to pick up the practice procedures and get to know the clients and their idiosyncrasies. Claiming damages for negligence was unheard of and the worst that could happen would be the loss of a client. Mind you, that could be disastrous in country practices, where not only the loss of a client, but also the loss of goodwill in a farming community could take years to rectify; the same applied to our heavy horse practice, so that after my arrival, I spent the first few days going round the stables with the 'Old Man' and just listening to him. He was greatly respected and had built up his reputation over many years. A major mistake on my part could not only lose the client, but could result in the client asking for Mr. Stanley by name, or even asking that I was not to be sent! A very humiliating experience which, fortunately, did not happen very often.

I was very lucky in that everyone in the practice helped me to settle in. I had, of course, 'seen practice' there as a student, but the qualification now put me on a higher footing, although there never was any hierarchical feeling within the staff.

* * * * * * * * * * * * *

That first week alone with the 'Old Man' taught me a lot, not only about how he worked, but about horses in general and heavy horses in particular. Each one had its own character; some were devious, some were just sly, but most were placid and docile and easy to get on with. In many cases, the horseman was more difficult than the horse.

Most of the large stables were in the Kings Cross and St. Pancras area, as that is where most of the coal came off the trains. One hundred years earlier, before trains, the stables would have been near the wharves by the river, or by the canals, as coal came in by boat at that time.

If the 'Old Man' had me well under his thumb when I was acting as his chauffeur, he had the horse keepers completely subservient. We would drive into the yard, he would lean out of the car window, give a kind of wolf whistle and sit back and wait for the horse driver to appear.

Most times, he would diagnose the cause of the

lameness, if that was the reason for the visit, by having the horse turned round in the stable; he did not require the animal to be trotted 'up and down', as we lesser mortals would require. His deafness sometimes caused problems. Frequently, he would issue his instructions and quickly turn away without realising that the horseman was asking for further advice or making some general comment. This left the impression that he was rude, when really he was not. In fact, he was as gentle with people as he was with his patients. As to the horsemen, some he had a general fondness for, but others, and these were the 'chancers', he had no time for at all. I think he disliked them, as he felt the animals might suffer for their lack of real interest in their charges.

The Old Man genuinely disliked one man in the King's Cross stables and he was not a man to hide his feelings. I never got to know his name, as he was always referred to as "the bloody fool".

My first meeting with him was not a very auspicious one. We arrived at the Rickett Cockerall horse hospital one cold morning in mid-winter and a large shire was brought out walking quite soundly.

"What's the matter with him?" asked the 'Old Man' gruffly.

"It's got snot running out of its snart", replied the horse-keeper in his broad cockney accent.

"What's he say?"

Before I could reply, the symptoms were repeated.

"It's got snot running out of its snart".

"What's he say?"

I was not quite so insensitive and quickly had to decide whether to snub the man and say that it had got a nasal discharge or whether to be polite to the man who seemed to show no sign of intimidation by the 'Old Man'. There was an obvious antagonism between them.

I decided on the latter.

"It's got snot running out of its snout", I compromised.

"Bloody fool". Was all I got and the 'Old Man'

walked away.

I was left to deal with the animal and prescribed a 'NUMBER ONE'.

A more embarrassing event occurred some time later. We arrived, as usual, at the King's Cross stables to make a routine call only to find that one of the members of the coal company's family [he had received his Knighthood for some conspicuous deed] was talking to one of the horse keepers. He introduced himself to Mr. Broad, emphasising the 'Sir' aspect of his name.

The 'Old Man' looked at him disdainfully. The Knight was showing signs of intimidation already, but with a slight obsequious gesture, held his hand out for a handshake. The 'Old Man' obliged. They had a short discussion as to what ailment we were treating and the client was given a brief account of what was to be done.

The 'Old Man' handed a bottle of 'NUMBER ONE' to the horse-keeper, but the Company Chairman, for that's who he was, intervened and took the bottle.

It must have been nervousness that made him shake the bottle violently with the result that the cork flew off and the drench shot all over the Old Man's serge coat.

The 'Old Man' knew what the result would be; the saturated solution of Epsom salts would dry immediately and leave the coat stiffened with the salt crystals – it would take some considerable effort to return it to normal.

"Bloody fool", said the 'Old Man' and stomped back to the car. We never saw the Chairman again.

Life in the horse part of the practice was happy and life with the cockney drivers always worth a laugh.
When the 'Old Man' retired, I was left to cope with the travelling around London to do the horse work. I often found myself having problems finding the more obscure stables and asked for the directions from other stable men.

One set of directions went like this, although it is impossible to be accurate with names.

"Go out of the stables and turn left. When you get to

'The Rose and Crown', turn right.

Go straight on past a urinal on the left and take the next left turn until you come to the 'Barley Mow'.

Turn right there until you see the next urinal on the left and take the next left turn.

Go past the 'Queen Elizabeth', past the next urinal in the centre of the road until you see the 'Crown and Anchor' on the left.

You will see a urinal on the corner. If you turn left there, you will see the stables".

One would be surprised how efficient that type of instruction turned out to be.

The same horseman gave me further instruction of a different nature.

Seeing me smoking one day, he told me a guaranteed way of stopping smoking. I was assured that his method would cure any smoking addict, but only if the smoker would be prepared to co-operate in full.

"Get two ordinary cigarettes without filters, get a long needle and four hairs from a horse's tail. Thread two of these hairs through the tobacco in each cigarette. Cut the ends off the hairs and insist the smoker must smoke both cigarettes completely and one straight after the other.

If he feels sick, he must still carry on smoking.

After the second cigarette he will never want to smoke again".

I am sure that the directions were given and emphasised with a few additional expletives, but that was the gist of his instructions.

I never tried it, but it sounds nauseating enough to work. Now, I suppose it would be regarded as 'aversion therapy'.

* * * * * * * * * * * * * *

Like any professional work, there are always periods of monotony, but quite suddenly things can change. A year after joining the practice, the horse population of London was hit with an Equine Flu epidemic, which meant that the hospitals were full of coughing horses. The fear was that pneumonia would develop and animals would either die or become a financial liability due to chronic lung damage. For me, it meant getting up at five in the morning, making dozens of bottles of all the types of horse drenches, being given new addresses to visit and having no time for meals. The epidemic lasted for some weeks. Most animals recovered quickly, some became long-term patients and others developed 'Strangles', a disease of horses, which, more often then not, resulted in abscesses in the throat. The only treatment for these was to lance the abscesses and drain the pus out. It was a testing time, but very rewarding when seeing the results of one's labour with the horses back on the road again.

Visiting the stables at night, when all the animals were in, was perhaps not what the casual visitor would expect. Each animal would have a chain from its collar passing through a ring on the wall. The length of chain would enable the animal to lay down and get up when it chose. But, like all large animals, being down for too long would result in chest congestion, so it was quite normal for the horses in the stable to keep rising and resting at very frequent intervals. Night-time in the stables was not a quiet affair: there was a continuous rattle of chains but this did not seem to affect the animals; they must have got used to it in time.

The horse practice continued well into the fifties, but the outcome was unstoppable.

WINKS AND WAGGING TAILS
St. Guinefort

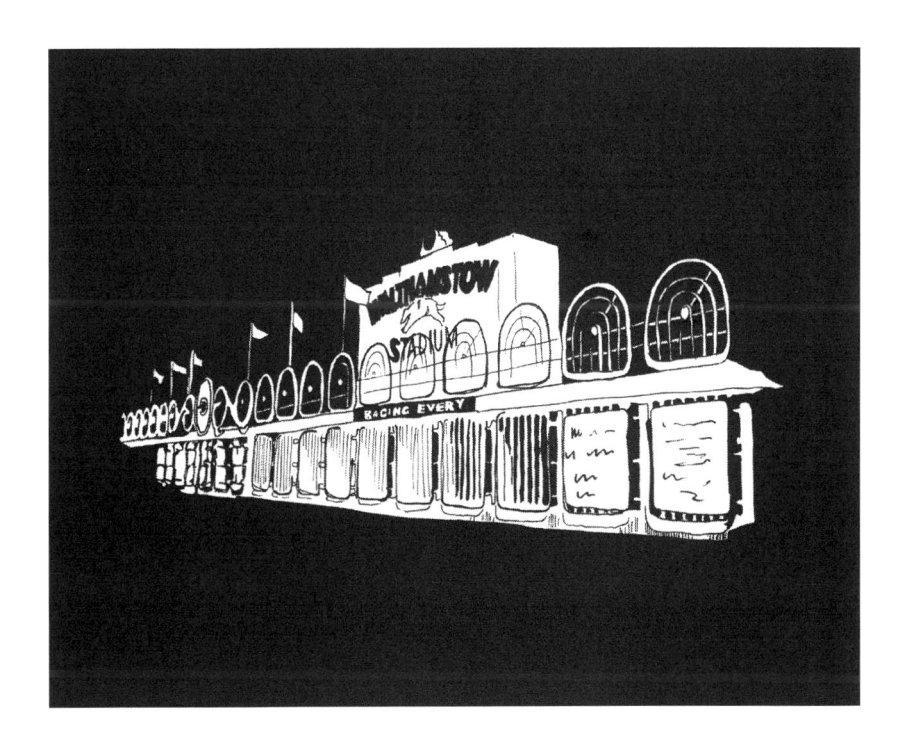

CHAPTER V

A DAY AT THE RACES

Many years ago, the Marx Brothers made a film with the title "A Day at the Races". As one would expect, it was a farcical day at a horse racetrack and one could sit back and enjoy the humour.

My day at the races may have been humorous to some, but to me it was a nightmare, which persisted in my mind for many years.

The races in this case were greyhound races.

As a student, I thought that it would be good to get experience in all aspects of possible veterinary work, and so I decided that I should have an idea as to the obligations of the veterinary surgeon at a greyhound race meeting.

The people in Craven Terrace, where I was 'seeing practice' at the time, suggested I contact a veterinary surgeon, who also had his practice north of Hyde Park, but who only dealt with small animals. I telephoned him and he seemed quite well disposed to taking me to the greyhound track, for which he was the official vet. In retrospect, I think he was delighted to have me with him for non-veterinary reasons!

The track was at Walthamstow and there was a meeting the following Tuesday evening.

I arranged to meet him at his surgery about 3 o'clock and accompany him to the track.

* * * * * * * * * * * * * *

Greyhounds are very nice animals and I have found them always easy to handle and treat. Nevertheless, they have a hunting background and there is always the instinct of hunting somewhere in their brain. This instinct seems to be implanted in the brains of all hounds and has its dangers. Occasionally, as the practice in Craven Terrace was so close to Hyde Park, we would be asked to treat a small dog, very often a Pekingese that had been mauled by a greyhound. No doubt, the greyhound saw in its mind a potential prey and instinct would take over.

Greyhounds also have a unique place in Christian theology.

In the thirteenth century, there developed a story which resulted in a greyhound being canonized, becoming known as

St Guinefort.

The story on which the greyhound became famous is simple.

The setting is a castle or manor in a district north of Lyons in France. The lady of the house had given birth to a baby son. One day, the master of the castle and his mistress left the baby in a cot, in a room, with a nurse in attendance. He also left his greyhound with the baby who was asleep. The greyhound was to guard the baby. In due course, the nurse left the baby alone with the greyhound. Some time later, a wolf entered the castle and was about to attack the baby, but was immediately challenged by the greyhound. A fierce fight followed and ultimately the wolf was killed. During the fight, the cot was overturned and the baby rolled under a table. The room, floor and cot were splattered with blood.

Some time later, the nurse returned to see the greyhound's mouth and body covered with blood and the baby missing. She was horrified and called the master, who had just returned and who immediately accused the dog and killed it.

Only later, when the baby was found alive and well, did he discover his dreadful error and, out of respect for the hound, had it ceremoniously buried in a well nearby.

The local population heard of the tragic event and came to worship the martyred greyhound, which became known as St Guinefort.

The greyhound's fame spread throughout the area and, in time, the local women would bring their children to the greyhound's grave for protection from disease and to ask the Saint to intercede and help to cure those children who were sick. This cult persisted for centuries and was still practiced in the twentieth century, despite being rejected by the Church.

Two other aspects of the Saint's personality were recorded at the time. Statues were made and one such effigy responded in two ways. Firstly, the movements of the greyhound's tail indicated to the pilgrims that their prayers were being answered.

But this wagging of its tail had a more realistic meaning; it was a sign of encouragement to men whose virility was troubling them. Secondly, the statue of the Saint was said to wink at young girls who wanted a husband, the wink signifying that their wishes would come true.

It was on the basis of this story that I decided that an apt title for these reminiscences should be 'Winks and Wagging Tails'.

* * * * * * * * * * *

To return to my day at the races, I found myself in Central London knocking on the door of the practice anticipating an interesting evening.

It turned out that the Vet did not have a car, so we trudged to Paddington Underground Station and, in due course, got on an Overground train to Walthamstow. We rattled along, but there was not much conversation between us; he seemed slightly vague and smelled more than slightly of alcohol.

In those days, the underground trains had not extended far out of London and the local suburban railway trains were old and decrepit.

The Overground Light Railway Station at Walthamstow was some distance from the racetrack, but there was no indication that we should hail a taxi and so we set out to walk. The weather was mild, as it was in the early days of autumn. Soon however, we were lucky enough to get a lift from one of my host's friends.

We arrived at a red brick building, which seemed to be teeming with men, all hurrying about as if there was no time to lose. I was introduced to a few people and then to the manager of the track. On the whole, the office area was a bit tatty and the general atmosphere somewhat unfriendly and preoccupied.

Even so, the manager gave me the impression that he was pleased to see me and greeted the Vet with a sense of relief, as if he had entertained doubts as to whether he would arrive. The Vet cheered up and immediately got down to business – in this case, to make a bee-line for the bar and knock back a couple of whiskies. He then placed a couple of bets on the first two races and knocked back another two whiskies. Even to my untrained mind, betting on dogs that you were vetting seemed a little extraordinary, but I could not intervene as I was merely a spectator, or so I thought.

We were now about half an hour from the start of the first race and he asked me to accompany him to the paddock. The paddock was a small concrete-floored area with a wired front and contained the six hounds, which had been entered for the first race. The hounds were jumping around, barking furiously, and appeared to be highly excited.

Soon arc lights around the track were switched on and the spectators suddenly went quiet.

Trumpets were sounded, obviously from a gramophone, and a row of men marched on to the arena, each with his greyhound. It would seem that the ritual had started. The handlers wore white coats and bowler hats. The hounds were colourful with their coats on and were more subdued now than when they had been in the paddock.

My Vet walked onto the track. He was wearing a brown overall type of coat that he had brought with him and donned a bowler hat; he gave the impression that he was making some sort of examination of the hounds. The bowler hat, which he had not brought with him, did not fit well, but he had quickly removed it by the time he returned to the office. A quick chat with the manager and then back to the bar.

Unfortunately, I didn't take too much notice as to what he did when he examined the hounds, but I joined in the excitement of the crowd as the hounds were put in their traps. More trumpets sounded, a shout went up and they were off.

The excitement of the race was marred somewhat as I was getting definitely uneasy; the Vet had now collapsed on a settee in the manager's office and was quite definitely drunk.

About that time in the mid-forties, there developed a rather disturbing gang warfare centred around greyhound racing, and there were reports in the papers that certain members of the gangs would go on the rampage, if the results of the races were not to their satisfaction. This had not worried me as I considered myself only on the fringe of the activities.

Preparations for the next race were starting and it was beginning to dawn on me, why my Vet had been so complacent about me accompanying him to the meeting: he was able to indulge, knowing that there was a 'back-up' to support him.

I stood back, trying to be as inconspicuous as possible, but was quickly approached by the manager saying I would have to take over. This did not seem to worry him at all.

My protestations were ignored: I explained that I was on my first visit to a greyhound meeting and that I was only a student.

That cut no ice: time was getting short and I had no alternative but to go with the manager to the paddock to see the next race's participants. One of the dogs was quite lame and lifted a hind leg every two or three steps.

"That one is lame", I declared with some authority, "it can't run".

"Too late", said the manager, "once they get to this stage they can't be withdrawn".

I'd no idea if he was right or wrong, but I was in no position to argue.

Once again, the trumpets sounded and the men in white coats and bowler hats appeared. I presumed the lame hound was one of the dogs, but was still led out for examination.

By then, I was dressed in the Vet's brown coat. As I was about a foot taller than he was, it didn't fit well and I found it difficult to button up. That was bad enough, but it got worse when I put on the official bowler hat, it was two sizes too small.

The arc lights, which had been switched on, left me nowhere to hide.

I was a new face and I seem to recall that the crowd let out quite a roar of appreciation. Whether the cheering was for a new face or whether it was for a rather stupid looking figure in a tight brown coat with a bowler hat perched on its head, I will never know, but it did give me some encouragement.

I now realized that I should have taken more notice of what had happened in the first race.

Anyhow, I stepped forward and approached the first hound. All of them were now barking fiercely and, instead of standing calmly as they did in the first race, they seemed to be joining in with the crowd. There was little risk of being bitten, as all the animals were wearing muzzles.

I remembered that, in the first race, the Vet had messed

about with their head end, so I decided, in a panic, that he must have been looking at their mouth and possibly looking to see if they had an inflamed throat.

Only those people who have tried to look down a dog's throat while it was wearing a muzzle will appreciate that it is not easy. All the help I got from the first handler was a gruff, "get a move on".

I tried to repeat this performance on each of the hounds, and the crowd was getting restless.

The spotlight dimmed, probably on the instruction of the manager as a way of getting me moving: the trumpets sounded again, the crowd became hushed and the dogs were put in their traps. I returned to the front of the stand and back to the manager's office, which overlooked the track, and waited.

The gates shot up and the dogs emerged, but unfortunately, two of them came out backwards.

Had they been put in backwards?

Was I supposed to check that as part of my duty?

Would the crowd go berserk?

Would the track be ransacked?

All of these questions raced through my mind but nothing happened, the crowd cheered lustily. I was relieved. The manager thanked me and told me to get ready for the next race. The Vet was still unconscious. This time, I was not interested in looking at the animals in the paddock, as I knew that my comments would be ignored anyway.

I stood back wondering how I would survive the remainder of the races.

The trumpets sounded again, the handlers appeared again and I now had the ordeal of being under the spotlight again. Would I get booed?

The cheer that I got after my first race seemed different from the cheer I received after the second race.

There was a marked difference in the attitude of the crowd, or at least some part of the crowd. I was met with a loud cheer of appreciation and not the cheer of derision as I had expected: everyone seemed to be delighted to see me again.

I got through the remainder of the races with a sense of achievement – in fact, I was quite proud of my performance.

By the time that all the races had been run I was getting into the atmosphere of greyhound racing. Odd people shook my hand, the manager thanked me very much, but did not recompense me for my help. There was no rampaging or people looking for my blood, the right dogs had won and the gangs were contented.

The Vet was still semiconscious but beginning to come round. I offered no help. I had taken over from him and that was enough for one evening. I was certainly not going to get him back to central London.

I made my way to the station with the crowd: no one recognised me and I slowly sauntered back to Craven Terrace. In a couple of days, the euphoria had passed and I never went to a greyhound track again; to this day I have no idea what I was supposed to look for when examining the hounds under the spotlight.

I never heard from the Vet again. I presume he must have returned home safely; nor did I discover whether he had backed the winning dogs in the first two races. I didn't really care. However, I learned two important lessons. Firstly, never trust your superiors and secondly, never trust your inferiors. The Vet had let me down and the handlers had offered no help. Being the official veterinary surgeon at a greyhound track was not for me.

London was still under nightly bombardment, but life went on as usual and boredom was never a problem at Craven Terrace.

THE BOMB

"The descent of man"
Charles Darwin

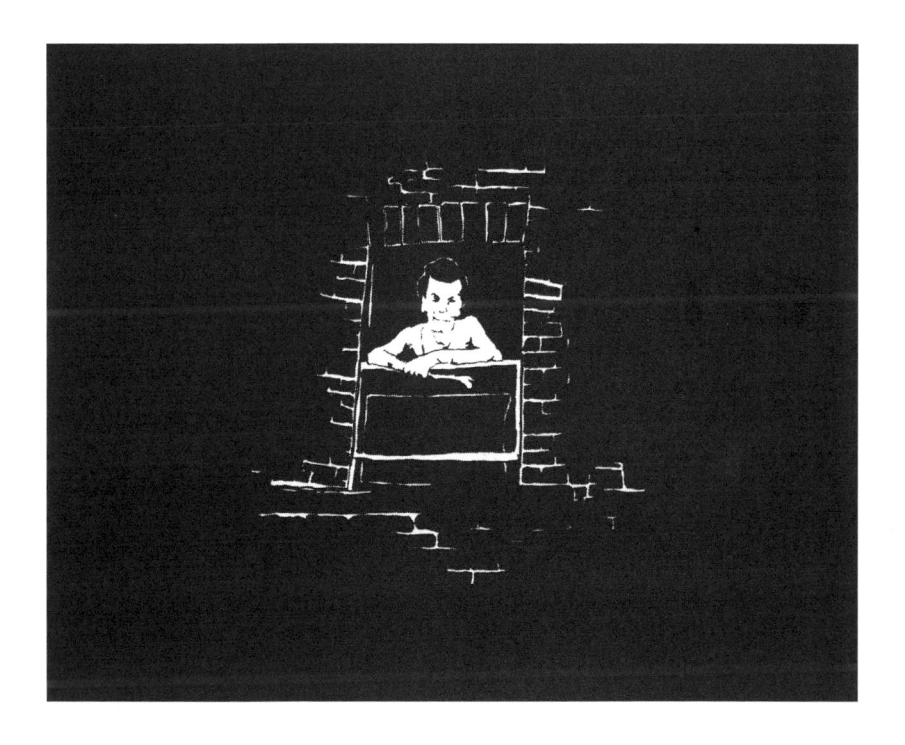

CHAPTER VI

THE BOMB

I was once again 'seeing practice' in Craven Terrace during the summer holidays. London was a dangerous place to live in, but so many people had to endure these dangers that, to join them, did not seem any hardship.

The war was still being waged at a serious level. London was the main target and was being bombed mercilessly. Every night was a nightmare of bombing, air raid sirens blasting the night, searchlights piercing the night sky, weaving their criss-cross patterns. Suddenly their bright, clear-cut rays would end in a blur, as they hit a low cloud, but generally fading out as the strength of the beam got lost into obscurity. Anti-aircraft guns were blazing away in the hope of hitting an enemy plane or, at least, scaring them off, so that they would not reach their target for the night. Barrage balloons were always flying to deter low flying bombers getting closer to their objective.

At the sound of the sirens, those people, who did not wish to spend their nights in the Underground made their way to their own small shelters with thermos flasks and sandwiches and hoped for the best. They would know if a bomb landed nearby and would leave their haven the next morning hoping that, if a bomb had dropped nearby, it was someone else's buildings that had been hit. All of this was commonplace at Craven Terrace, as it was only about a hundred yards from Hyde Park, which was the centre of numerous anti-aircraft gun sites and barrage balloons and searchlight detachments. More often than not, shrapnel from the guns would scatter on pavements and the roofs of the houses in the area and the pavements and yards would be swept clean the next morning.

A bomb had fallen on the corner of Brook Street and Brook Mews some two years previously in the early days of bombing. The site had been partly cleaned up and levelled, so as not to leave any obvious danger to children who might use it as a playground, although most children had already been evacuated. In the summer, it was dusty and this provided some soil for patches of weed and 'London Pride' trying to overcome war's disruptions. Piles of bricks, many bound together with cement, made it a hazard to walk over and, anyhow, it was not a short cut to anywhere. In the winter, it was muddy and even less inviting to the pedestrian then in the summer.

Lancaster Gate was not an obvious target for German bombers, it was far enough from the City; it was nowhere near the river, which was a common route indicator for night bombers when the moon was up and, with the exception of Paddington Station, was void of vital war activity.

Nevertheless, the ARP was being stretched, but on blank days it was putting in as much practice as possible, as new recruits were being enlisted all the time. The head of the ARP made himself known to us from time to time, as he seemed perturbed that, if a bomb landed on the kennels, he would be in a quandary as to how he would cope with nervous dogs and cats that may have escaped from the boarding kennels. Being a retired ex-army captain, he could well cope with hysterical people by giving a few sharp orders, but dumb animals were a potential problem. His answer to this, he thought, would be to hold an exercise with a mock bomb landing near the kennels. The exercise was to be on a Saturday afternoon, when normal daily work routines would not be interrupted too much.

The 'Bomb' would land at the junction of Brook Mews North and Craven Terrace, more or less where the original bomb had landed and a large chalk circle would indicate the size of the crater – no traffic would be allowed to enter this area. At the time of the first real bomb, there had been no damage to the occupied kennels, so the Captain had no experienced member under his control to give advice. This time, the kennels would be damaged and the flat occupied by Jack and Jane would be declared unsafe.

The Captain had an added incentive to hold an exercise; he had recently been allocated a new piece of evacuation equipment, somewhat like a breeches buoy [a contraption often used at sea to transport injured seamen from boat to shore or from one ship to another], and he was keen to get this tried out as soon as possible. The equipment was packed in a large canvas bag with an outside pocket containing printed instructions. The bag was left in the kennels several days before the day in which the 'Bomb' was due to fall.

By now, the Captain had lost interest in the escaped animal problem and was centred on his new 'toy'.

The Captain's decision was to assume that someone in Jack's flat would be injured and should be lowered out of the window to safety by using this new contraption. Jane quickly made it known that no stranger was going to be allowed into her new flat and particularly into her conjugal bedroom. On top of that, she was certainly not going to be lowered out of the window for all to see.

"It's not going to be me either," said Jack emphatically, even before he had been asked. He seemed to have a premonition.

The Captain was not going to argue with Jack. Normally, he would have issued an order and that would have been the end of the matter, but he had met too many cockneys in the last few years to expect any response to an outright order, and 20 years in the army had not taught him the delicacies of persuasion. Perhaps that was why he had never persuaded anyone to promote him above the rank of Captain.

"But this would be for the good of the country", he said weakly to Jack, hating the implication that he was pleading.
"Think about it", was all he could say. He balked at saying "Please", and only just avoided "Man" after the "Think about it".

Jack thought about it and said "No".

The main topic of conversation over the next few days in the surgery was the 'Bomb' and what would develop on the Saturday after next. At the same time, there was a subtle war being waged with Jack to get him to acquiesce to his potential heroism and becoming the 'centre of attraction'. Nobody really knew what the new lowering contraption would be like, but all, except Jack, fancied an interesting afternoon's activity. We all thought that Jack should agree, not for the good of the community, but for the fun that we would all have, as he was coming round to the idea of being somewhat of a hero and his self esteem was gradually rising.

Jane was not happy, but a further visit of the Captain to the practice with a more pleading and patriotic approach seemed to be winning Jack over and Jane would agree in the end. The Captain visualised success and became even obsequious in his discussions with Jane. He knew that he had won Jack over.

Jane would agree with her new husband.

She was not a hundred percent satisfied, but finally conceded that the exercise should go ahead.

At last, everything had been decided.

At 2.30 on the Saturday afternoon, the 'Bomb' would land and chaos would reign. This would last only until the ARP arrived and then, according to the Captain, everything would be all right. Dealing with chaos was his speciality, particularly if he was the organiser of the chaos in the first place.

At 2.30 precisely the 'Bomb' dropped.

A chalk circle was drawn in the road and a uniformed man guarded it. The start was not auspicious, a motor cyclist drove down Brook Street and was halted by the crater guard.

"You can't pass here".

"Why not?" was the rather irate reply.

"There's a bomb crater just here".

"Balls", said the motorcyclist and drove over the crater. He had no intention of wasting his precious petrol ration by driving round Lancaster Gate.

In the meantime, preparations were being made for the lowering of Jack from the bedroom window of his flat. Two ARP wardens with tin hats and arm bands were in the room with somewhat less self confidence than the Captain had originally shown. The Captain had not yet turned up. Jack was in the room with Jane and already beginning to rue his decision to cooperate. When the Captain did arrive, he decided that a bit of realism was required. This being so, he told Jack that the explosion had resulted in Jack breaking his femur. Jack now had to lie on the floor of his bedroom and had a long wooden splint put on his leg. This extended from armpit to foot and both legs would be bound together. Jack was beginning to show signs of real shock. Jane was fussing around trying to overcome a fear of an approaching catastrophe.

At last, Jack was on the bedroom floor with the long wooden splint in place and both legs bound together with strips of khaki-coloured bandage. He was gently rolled off the floor onto a canvas stretcher, which had wooden poles at each side. The bedroom window was not high, but the yard outside was quite short so that the angle of descent was about 45 degrees. This seemed not to disturb the ambulance man, who was in charge of the lowering device. Ropes were lowered to the yard and were picked up by four volunteers from the mews. At the same time, two more volunteers had arrived in the bedroom to help the two ARP men with the ropes.

Jane was getting more concerned, as there were now four strangers in the bedroom, as well as herself and Jack.

"Be careful", she kept repeating, a remark aimed at the ARP men.

Jack, who was now immobilised and could only see the ceiling and the electric light thought she was speaking to him.

"How can I be bloody careful?" His confidence was waning.

"I can't bloody well move." Jack was not a prolific swearer, so this indicated his concern.

Mr. Widden and I were watching from the dispensary door, ready to help if necessary. It was a quiet Saturday, there were no calls and we had been looking forward to this for some days. The windows of houses in the mews and at the back of Craven Terrace were now crowded with people, producing the odd bit of banter. News had spread that something interesting could happen and this broke the monotony of a Saturday afternoon.

Up in Jack's bedroom, a label had been attached round Jack's neck saying simply: 'Simple fracture of right femur'.

Small loops were attached to the handles of the stretcher and these threaded through four small pulley wheels on the lowering ropes. A final rope was attached to the end of the stretcher to act as a restraint, so that the stretcher could drop at the required speed.

All seemed to be going well, the written instructions had been followed to the 'T'. Nevertheless, one vital piece of information was lacking, i.e. which way the injured party was to be lowered down. Jack had been strapped to the stretcher with his head towards the window and, although there was some discussion as to which was the best way to lower him, the decision was made for them by the fact that the bedroom was so full of people and so small that he could not be turned round anyway.

Jack was to be lowered head first from the bedroom window.

He didn't fancy that, but there was so much noise in the room with the result that nobody heard his now feeble complaints; he couldn't move to point out the dangers.

The stretcher was fastened to the pulleys and eased up towards the window.
Jack appeared headfirst from the window. A cheer went up from all the spectator windows and Jack gave a mental majestic wave to his supporters.

The foot of the stretcher was raised up by the volunteers; they got it to an angle of 45 degrees by raising their end above their heads. Jack slid forward about six inches, as his feet were raised. He thought he was doomed and uttered a long drawn out "Stop".

He was firmly strapped in, however, and this movement was a settling in process.

The stretcher began moving with what was meant to be a slow descent. The volunteers in the yard took the strain. Jack had gone a deathly pale and could well have been taken for a corpse. Jane was panicking and still pleading, "Be careful".

The angle of 45 degrees made control very difficult. Jack, together with the weight of the stretcher and ropes was heavier than expected; the ropes began to sag and Jack began to sway. He was now trying to sit up and somehow escape, but that added more strain to the volunteers. Mr. Widden and I saw impending trouble and each took a rope at the yard end, but there was no extra help in the bedroom. The volunteers were weakening and the two on the left side were being forced to the window like a losing tug-of-war team.

Within seconds, their grip had lost all its power, and with the dread of being sucked out of the window, they let go. Jack was still six feet, headfirst, from the ground. The other two men upstairs on the right rope could not take the load and they also let go. Jack hit the ground with a thud. He landed on the splinted 'fractured leg' side and let out a loud yell and numerous oaths. Jane was leaning out of the window swearing louder than Jack. The four culprits in the bedroom were heading downstairs for the pub and the yard was full of anguished ARP men.

Mr. Widden took control and managed to get Jack to quieten down. Jack stopped shouting and just groaned.

It was some ten minutes later, when Jack had been untangled from the ropes and released from the stretcher, but still lying on the cold concrete, unable to move because of the splint, that Mr. Widden realised that Jack had broken his right arm. Ambulance men were called in and the fractured arm bandaged to the leg splint, which was still in position and could not be moved without causing Jack severe pain. Jack was back on the stretcher again.

The audience had sensed tragedy and all, except the intoxicated ones, had gone quiet. The drunks carried on cheering and drinking more beer. This was better than the cinema. The others drifted away from their windows.

It was decided that Jack should be rushed to St. Mary's Hospital down the road by ambulance as soon as one could be summoned.

By this time, the Captain had arrived and, as in good army fashion, was deciding who should take the blame. As he saw himself as the CO, it was his duty to take charge and a few words to the injured party would help. He was well trained at offering comfort to the less well off and pushed his way to Jack's resting place on the yard floor. With a gesture of deep condolence he leaned over Jack to offer comfort. He leaned over too far. His tin hat fell forward, the strap slid off his chin and the hat hit Jack, rim first on the bridge of his nose. Jack let out a half yell, half scream and nearly passed out. To go with his fractured arm, he now had a broken nose. The officer saw defeat staring him straight in the eye.

"Get him to hospital"!

He took his tin hat, put it under his arm and walked away like an undertaker, who had just passed the body to the priest at a funeral.

An ambulance was called from the odd array of transport that was waiting in Brook Street. It arrived at the 'crater', only to be halted by the guard who was still diverting what traffic there was.

"You can't come this way, there's a crater here".

The guard was unaware of the calamity in the yard behind the kennels. He had heard the cheering and had assumed that all had gone well and soon the exercise would be over and he could go home. He didn't budge. The disgruntled ambulance driver thought the exercise was still on, so reluctantly turned his vehicle slowly round and headed back to the front entrance of the practice in Craven Terrace.

Jack, back on the stretcher, was now carried up the back stairs, head first again and was carried out of the front door and gently eased into the ambulance. I agreed to go to the hospital with him and Jane was left to clear up her bedroom with a promise that Mr Widden would drive her to the hospital, once Jack had been admitted.

Her last words to Jack were, "Be careful".

Jack groaned.

The ambulance's bell clanged, as we went up Praed Street to the emergency Department of St Mary's.

All was quiet, as there was no immediate bombing and, due to petrol rationing, motor accidents were rare. The emergency department would start to get busier after the pubs had closed.

Jack was carefully wheeled into a reception room and, within a few minutes, a young doctor arrived in a white coat and a new stethoscope wrapped purposely carelessly round his neck.

"What have we here?" He sounded like a pseudo expert on the 'Antiques Road Show'.

He quickly looked at the label round Jack's neck.

"Ah, a fractured femur, how did it happen?"

"It was the bomb in Brook Street". The ambulance man was trying to co-ordinate his thoughts – he had not been at the fiasco in the mews'yard.

"The bomb in Brook Street", repeated the Doctor. "I didn't hear a bomb, I wasn't warned that there had been a raid".

The Doctor had been left on his own and had not expected any serious decision-making on his shift.

"It wasn't a real raid", said the ambulance man.

"Wasn't a real raid", repeated the now perplexed doctor.

"It was a mock raid", said the ambulance man.

"A mock raid", said the Doctor, who seemed to have a habit of repeating everything that was said to him.

"Well, how did he fracture his femur?"

"It's not a fractured femur", said the ambulance man, who had taken it on himself to act as spokesman.

"It's a fractured humerus and broken nose".

"It says 'fractured femur' on the label", said the Doctor, who gave more credence to the written word than to the oral uttering of an apparent half-wit of an ambulance man.

"No, it's really a fractured humerus, we put the label on before he broke his arm".

The doctor, with a newly acquired MB, was having no truck with this man.

"Don't be stupid man, he has a splint on for a fractured femur; I'll have his leg X-rayed".

With that he started to briskly remove the bandage from Jack's broken arm.

Jack moaned.

"It's his arm that's broken, really it is", said the ambulance man.

"Don't be stupid man". A newly-qualified MB can call an ambulance man 'a stupid man'.

"I'll straighten his arm", still trying to remove the bandage.

Jack groaned in pain. "It's my bloody arm".

The Doctor was losing ground and felt that he must reinsert his authority.

"Why the hell did you put his leg in a splint if he has a broken arm?"

Normally he would not have said "Hell" but this was a special occasion.

"The leg was splinted first", muttered the ambulance man, "before he broke his arm".

The ambulance man was also losing ground and could only repeat himself.

The Doctor was losing more ground. "Why", you could see him thinking to himself, "would they put a man's leg in a splint, if they knew he was going to break his arm?"

"What about his nose?" The Doctor was trying to get back on firm ground. Broken noses he could deal with.

"The broken nose came later, after he had broken his arm".

"The broken nose came later", repeated the Doctor. Medical school had not trained him for this.

"Can I have a quiet word?" I said gently to the Doctor trying to help.

"Who are you? Are you a doctor?" He glared at me with a look of disdain.

I didn't like him much, so I just said, "I'm a Vet." I thought I could legitimately leave out 'student'; he was not much older than me anyway.

"A vet".

I came to the conclusion he was even less articulate than

I first thought.

"Yes", I said. "I was with him at the time", and I went on to try and explain what had happened. He seemed to understand.

Five years' training had not prepared him how to remove a leg splint from a man with a broken arm, and Jack was getting weak with pain.

The Doctor made one last effort to stamp his authority on the proceedings; he dabbed a piece of lint on Jack's nose.

Jack groaned and passed out.

The doctor was nearly as pale as Jack and left without another word.

"I'm getting out of this", said the ambulance man as he hurried off.

I left Jack to be resuscitated and X-rayed by other medical staff, who had come to his rescue. They wheeled him out of sight.

I ambled slowly back to Craven Terrace and sanity.

Back home, everything was quiet; Jane was putting on a coat and heading for the hospital.
I tried to reassure her.
The ARP men had disappeared.
The Captain was never seen again.

There were no legal repercussions; those were the days before everybody seemed to want monetary reward for what happens in a normal world.

Jack received no counselling. His cockney background would be sufficient to see him through worse troubles than that.

It is hard to believe that, in some laboratory behind the examination room in the 'Accident and Emergency' area of St. Mary's Hospital, Fleming and his co-workers were undertaking fundamental research on the organism that was to lead to the production of Penicillin, which saved millions of human and animal lives., but life has its twists and turns.

MISTAKEN IDENTITY

"The man who makes no mistakes
does not usually make anything"
E.J. Phelps

CHAPTER VII

MISTAKEN IDENTITY

Most pet owners or farmers would affirm quite positively that they know their animals and could identify them anywhere.

This, however, is not necessarily the case and we tend to accept what is presented to us as fact. As Diogenes stated, "We think and believe what we want to believe and think".

In the dispensary at Craven Terrace, beneath the bank of mahogany drawers, was a cast iron fireplace, the residue from a past 'below stairs' living accommodation, probably servants' quarters.

No real fire was ever lit there in my time in the practice and it remained part of the décor. It did, on one occasion, provide a 'bolt-hole' for a cat, which probably recalled its previous visit when it suffered the indignity of castration, although this visit was merely to check its teeth. With both doors closed, Jack felt that there was no immediate probability of escape and left the rather nervous cat unattended, sitting on the table.

The cat had other ideas; it jumped from the table, took a quick look round the room and shot up the chimney. As this was the basement of a five-storey building, there seemed every possibility that, in due course, the cat would come down.

All three of us, Jack, Mr Widden and myself, knelt down in front of the fireplace convinced that our friendly calling 'pussy', 'pussy', 'pussy' would bring it down, but there was neither sight nor sound of it. We wondered how far up it would have got. The fireplace in Mr Widden's lounge was used in the winter, but this was summertime. We didn't know if Mrs. Matthews ever lit a fire, but we warned her to keep any cat that came out of her fire-place until we could collect it. However, none appeared. My bedroom fireplace was blocked off.

The cat, which was completely black, was owned by the butcher, who lived above his shop at the end of the Terrace. He was a friendly sort of man, or appeared to be, when he left the cat on the rare occasions that it needed attention. Also, Mrs Widden was a customer of his.

Bowls of milk and meat were put in the hearth but proved useless.

Towards the end of surgery, the owner arrived and Mr Widden took on the task of telling him of the very regrettable disappearance. Jack and I waited anxiously for the outcome of the conversation, which seemed to be taking too long a time for comfort. However, the butcher was not very concerned and Mr. Widden gathered the impression that, as it was his wife's pet anyway, he was quite pleased to see it go. Maybe the cat got more attention and love than he did. He went home, quite cheerfully, to tell his wife what had happened and mitigated the disaster by saying that Mr. Widden thought it would probably turn up in a day or so. This proved not to be the case; time went by and the episode was forgotten.

Some weeks later, we found the butcher in the waiting room with his cat in a basket, saying it had turned up in the street the previous day and could we check it over? We never saw the butcher's wife but, according to her husband, she was delighted with the return of her pet.

We were all delighted, especially Jack, and this time there was no risk of an escape, as the chimney had been blocked by a piece of plywood.

Mr Widden checked the cat and then turned to Jack.

"Wasn't the butcher's cat a castrated tom?"

"Yes", said Jack, "that's what it came in for on the first visit".

"This one is a female"

This left us in a quandary as to what to tell the butcher, but in the end, we all agreed that he must be told the truth.

The cat was checked out and taken back to the owner.

"This is not your wife's cat", he was told; "this is a female".

The butcher seemed unperturbed and was quite happy to let things stand.

He really didn't care one way or the other; his wife was happy and the household was back to normal again.

His parting remarks were: "I won't tell the wife and for God's sake, don't you tell her, she is convinced this is her cat and she insists that it even remembers its name. Lets keep it quiet and forget it."

The butcher returned home happy, the wife was delighted and the practice was relieved.

We did, nevertheless, have an underlying fear that, in the

not too distant future, the 'castrated tom' would be returned with a basket of kittens.

In the end, when no kittens turned up, we came to the conclusion that the 'new' cat had been spayed and we were in the clear.

* * * * * * * * * * * * * *

Some years later, in different circumstances and with an unknown conclusion, an identity problem occurred.

I was undertaking research in the 'Fading Puppy' syndrome, trying to identify why certain bitches produced litters, which died soon after birth. One particular kennel near Carlisle had this syndrome in their brood bitches, and, from time to time, they would put one of their bitches in a basket and put it on the night train to London. I would be duly warned and would be waiting at the station to collect it, take it to the lab. There I would collect a sterile urine sample and put the dog back on the train the next day.

One particular morning I arrived at the station, having been alerted that the bitch was on the night train, and waited for the train, but no dog.

I checked and rechecked with the man on the station and looked carefully at all the luggage that was spread out on the platform. There was no basket and no dog. I duly left, assuming it would be on the next train but leaving my 'phone number if there was anything to report.

An hour or so later, well before the next train was due in, I got a call to say they had found the dog in its basket and could I collect it, as it was barking furiously. Animals in baskets always attract onlookers and I was concerned that too many questions would be asked as to the dog's ultimate destination. The anti-vivisectionists would make the most of it, although no one was going to experiment on it.

I rushed over and saw the same man at the station and got some sort of apology out of him, but he attempted to defuse the situation by saying he had taken the dog out of the basket to give it a drink of milk.

This appalled me.

"Never take an animal out of its cage or basket", I told him, "it might have escaped". I had in mind the butcher's cat.

"You're right", he said, "I remember last year, when there were several cats arriving at the station for the big cat show: I took one of the cats, which was kicking up a fuss, out of its cage to give it a drink of milk, and it bolted up the platform like a cat out of Hell."

"Good Lord", I said, "what did you do?"

"Oh", he replied with a smug look of satisfaction, knowing that he was going to be congratulated for his burst of inspiration. "We never saw the cat again, so I caught one of the station's wild cats, popped it in the basket and went off duty.

Under no circumstances could this have had a happy ending, but we can only conjecture all the permutations that might have arisen. Was the owner of the cat horrified, when she opened the basket expecting a prize Persian or Siamese, only to see a mongrel 'moggy' staring at her? Was the new owner under the impression that the previous owner was trying to sell her a dud? I kept clear of St. Pancras Station for a while.

* * * * * * * * * * * * *

It may be easy to understand that two black cats could be difficult to separate in the mind of an owner, who is mentally geared to hope for a positive result. It is less easy to understand how two different breeds of dogs could be the subject of mistaken identity, but it happens.

In the summer months, dogs of varying breeds are trimmed or clipped to rid them of a thick coat and the discomfort in the heat of sunny days.

Jack earned the practice additional income by doing the necessary beauty treatment: hair shampooing, clipping and trimming together with nail clipping and ear plucking.

As many as six or seven dogs may be subject to this indignity in one day. After clipping, the dogs would be driven over to the kennels in Star Street and left there for a few hours to avoid overcrowding in the kennels in Craven Terrace.

Towards evening in the normal surgery hours, owners would call to collect their pets.

One such owner arrived, gave his name, and one of us motored to Star Street and returned with the appropriate canine.

The dog was taken up to the waiting owner, who was presented with his terrier: in this case, a Sealyham.

The dog seemed delighted to get out of the kennels and wagged its tail with delight and jumped up to greet the man now holding the lead. To the dog, the fact that his lead was on indicated that it was leaving the premises very shortly.

The owner, who, it would appear, had never had his dog clipped before, burst out laughing and remarked that the dog looked so different.

"I wouldn't believe that trimming would make the dog so different", he said. " I think he looks great".

He paid his fee, gave Jack a tip and left with an air of delight. The dog seemed to have the same opinion and both went on their way, with the dog fiercely wagging its tail and barking.

Some time later, another owner arrived and his dog was duly presented to him. But it wasn't his dog at all.

"My dog is a Sealyham", he said, "This is a Fox Terrier!"

"Are you sure? "asked Jack, which was rather an inane question.

"Of course I'm sure", said he owner, "Sealyhams have short legs, this one has long legs", which in turn was an equally inane answer.

The truth was beginning to dawn on Jack.

"I think we have made a mistake and some one else has taken your dog home, but don't worry, we will go and collect yours straight away".

Fortunately, we knew the address of the first owner and it was up to me to get into the car and try and sort out the problem.

I knocked on the door, it was opened and I said, "I think there has been some mistake and we gave you the wrong dog."

"That is our dog", said the puzzled owner pointing to an inside room.

"They want to take the dog", said the owner to his wife,

who had just walked in from the shops.

I was invited in and there was the Sealyham asleep on the mat in front of the fireplace.

"Of course its not Rex" said the wife in a derisory tone. "Don't say you brought the wrong dog home".

I sensed matrimonial problems, so decided to depart as quickly as possible.

This was a very amiable dog, which was quite happy to be woken up, put on a lead and taken into the car and exchanged for the Fox Terrier. The owner, who was also very amiable, took it all in his stride, grinned slyly, and was united with the real pet. He considered it a great joke and we left good friends.

The Sealyham was returned to its real owner, who was not quite so amicable, but left without offering Jack his tip.

All ended well and we remarked that not only had the first owner mistaken the identity of his dog, but the dog had mistaken the identity of his owner – they say that owners come to resemble their pets in appearance but, in this case, the unfriendly character of the real owner seemed not to equate with the friendly character of his pet.

* * * * * * * * * * * * *

Professor McCunn, my old anatomy Professor, told me, on one of my visits to him, of a more dramatic case of mistaken identity.

As a renowned animal expert, he had been appointed consultant to the menagerie, which was a permanent feature of Bertram Mills Circus at Olympia in London. He was required to make routine visits to the menagerie and check on the health of the animals.

He told me that recently two inspectors of one of the animal charities had called on him, both with very serious expressions.

"Professor", one said, " we feel it our duty to inform you that we are not satisfied with the conditions in which one of the exhibits was being kept".

Professor McCunn was not one to be easily frightened and, quite calmly, asked for details.

"It is the octopus, which we have been observing for some time now. It appears to be very ill. It has not been fed during our observations and has not moved for some days and is breathing slowly. We think it is dying and we will have to report back to head office with a possible prosecution. We felt it only polite to warn you".

The Professor stood up and thanked them and they started to leave.

"What should I have done Ablett?" he questioned me.

"In the end, I felt that I should be lenient with them and avoid embarrassment by explaining the facts to them".

"Come back gentlemen and take a seat.
I feel I must inform you that the octopus is, in reality, a rubber one. It is put at the bottom of its aquarium and placed over a small pump, which gives the appearance of very regular breathing. It has been there for months, and the public don't really expect an octopus to move."

The inspectors, with red faces, apologised for wasting the Professor's time and left. The Professor did not apologise as it was not in his nature, but he enjoyed the encounter as a future talking point to interested parties.

Not all aspects of mistaken identities involved animals. Sometimes, dishonesty does not pay and where dishonest mistakes occur, one can only relax and enjoy the pleasure of considering all the aspects that may have resulted from a criminal activity that goes wrong.

At one stage of my life in Craven Terrace, I had the luxury of being given a practice car in the form of an open top Morris Minor. On the day of the crime, the sun was blazing down, the air was warm and I folded up the canvas hood of the car and set out on my round of visits. Half way through the morning, I called on a terrier, which had suffered a few weeks of gastric and intestinal troubles. Things were not improving and I decided that I needed to do something more positive and prevent the owner from thinking that maybe she should go elsewhere. Before calling, I left her a message asking her to collect a sample of the dog's faeces, so that I could get a laboratory report on any abnormality.

Post-war England was a fairly honest place and one was not in the habit of anticipating car theft or vandalism: cars were rarely locked when unattended.

The dog in question was examined and the owner duly presented me with a faecal sample in an empty 'Milk Tray' chocolate box. I returned to the car, threw the box on the back seat before getting into the car.

I made the next call and returned to the car to find that the chocolate box was missing. Some passer-by had decided that a box of chocolates so easily available was too tempting to ignore.

Was the box given to a girl friend? Was it taken home and opened in front of the wireless after dinner? We shall never know, but the possible outcomes conjure up numerous intriguing situations that can only leave a sense of quiet satisfaction.

A similar event occurred in St Pancras Station. I had collected a small parcel, which had been sent by train from the kennels that were experiencing 'Fading Puppy' syndrome. The parcel, which contained a dead puppy, was wrapped in brown paper with my name on it, but no address. I collected it, went to a phone box to alert the lab. that I was on my way. Unfortunately, I left the parcel by the 'phone and went to the car. I quickly realized what I had done and went back to the 'phone box, but no parcel. Some one had seen it and taken it, no doubt hoping for a worthwhile prize. Again, one can only conjecture what the reaction would have been when the parcel was opened, only to discover a dead puppy.

Dishonesty sometimes gets its reward and when this occurs, we have no real sympathy with the perpetrator.

* * * * * * * * * * * * *

There are times when we expect a higher then normal level of integrity only to be disappointed when that higher level fails to materialize

We read of the story of the 'Good Samaritan' and are impressed by the concern one has for one's fellow men.

It was a typical hot August Saturday afternoon, very

much like it would have been when the traveller was walking from Jerusalem to Jericho. I was quite bored; the phone was silent and there was nothing to do except wait for tea and then wait for dinner. After dinner, it would be the usual Saturday evening radio programmes and then to bed. Mr. and Mrs Widden and the baby were out for the afternoon and evening and I was on duty for the rest of the day. The kitchen window was open, as the stifling heat of a summer heat-wave had penetrated every room in the house and seemed to have penetrated every square inch of Paddington; there was no traffic and not a soul in sight in the mews or in the short stretch of road between the church at one end and Craven Terrace at the other. Opening the window seemed to have let more heat into the house than cooling the air inside. I gazed at the scene two storeys below. The mews was silent, as the pub next door was now closed. Brook Mews looked more desolate than usual by being exposed on either side by the flattened bombed-out areas of rubble, sand and the odd tuft of desperate weed striving to survive in a hostile world. It could have been a view from one of the flat roofs in any Middle Eastern city with people laying out their prayer mats on the dry dusty adjoining roofs, if it hadn't been for the large grey stone church at the end of the street and its passage on the left-hand side, giving a short cut to Sussex Gardens.

Mental apathy had set in and the world seemed dead. A flicker of movement in the passageway to the left of the church dragged my gaze reluctantly towards it. That was the passageway, where occasionally a 'flasher' would be reported, but was never caught.

A bedraggled figure staggered into the hot sunlight and tottered across the footpath and into the road. Another drunk from one of the many pubs round Paddington Station was heading 'for God knows where', maybe for another pub, but by this time all the pubs would be closed. By the look of him, he would not know this. Maybe he was heading for home, wherever home was for this poor figure.

The only hazard was, that if he veered left, he would fall down the steps in Elms Mews.

Soon, he would have made the short distance to Craven

Terrace and would disappear out of sight. But he didn't make it to the end of the road; the staggering ceased after about twenty yards and he collapsed in a crumpled heap in the middle of the road and lay curled up, like a kitten, in the dust. An odd movement of the arms and legs showed he was still alive, but he made no attempt to get up. The heat had got him just as it had got me, and neither of us wanted to move.

What could I do anyway? A vague twinge of conscience suggested that I should get up and go and see if he was alright, but I knew he was out of this world and enjoying some drunken reverie, so best to leave him alone. Once committed, any action would result in my having to do something and what could one do with a drunk? Maybe the police would come and take him away. Better to sleep it off in the road than in a police cell. If I telephoned the police, I would probably be involved somehow and it was too hot to be involved. Maybe someone would come along and deal with him.

I lost interest and went back to dreaming.

Some time elapsed and a second figure emerged from the churchyard and headed towards Craven Terrace. This one was sober and with a purposeful step, which suddenly faltered when he saw the heap in the road. He was well dressed with his jacket over his shoulder and his sleeves rolled up. This, I thought, was a man of action who could cope with the situation and relieve me of any involvement. The purposeful step was resumed, and without any hesitation, he did a detour round the crumpled heap and continued without a backward glance and disappeared out of sight.

That worried me; the sleeping figure was still partly my responsibility as I had seen him first, but it was still too hot to go down three flights of stairs and out of the surgery to attend to a sleeping drunk. Anyhow, if one person had come by, why not another. I decided to wait and see.

There wasn't long to wait. Another figure appeared from the same shadow, but this time it was a woman, thirtyish and well-dressed, with a bag of shopping. She saw the figure lying in the road almost immediately and had no hesitation in turning round and heading straight back into the church passageway and going home the long way round via Craven Road.

No help to my conscience here either.

I came to a decision; I'll wait five minutes and then telephone the police. After all, he may be ill or may be choking, although the spasmodic movement of legs or arms showed he was still alive.
I was convinced in my own mind that once the five minutes had elapsed, I would talk myself into giving him a further five minutes.

Salvation arrived before the five minutes were up and this time in the form of the local vicar, in a black jacket and dog collar. He was a middle-aged man known only vaguely to me via the Widdens: tallish, greying hair and quite thin. He would know how to cope and what to do; it was his job to look after the fallen anyway. His response was a credit to his calling; he made straight for the reclining figure and leaned over him. I could tell from his attitude that he was talking earnestly to the figure and remonstrating with him by waving a finger at him and then pointing directly to the centre of the body. This didn't seem quite like the helping hand that I had expected, but he seemed to know what he was doing. I began to take a little more interest in what was going on. The figure was responding and, after a bit of a struggle, but without any help from the vicar, managed to reach a half sitting position. The vicar continued to point at him but not to his face, as one would imagine from a man of the church, who would be expected to be giving some sort of sermon on the evils of drink, before giving the helping hand to get him on his feet again.
He seemed to be pointing towards his abdomen.
I could now see quite clearly that the poor victim of drink was not trying to get to his feet, but was fumbling with his trousers trying to button up his flies. The vicar persisted

with his remonstrations in a very positive way, with his finger emphasising his words of command. The drunk persisted with his fumbling, trying to get the buttons done up as quickly as possible, so that he could get back to sleep again. This lasted several more minutes, until the vicar was satisfied that all was safely gathered in and, with a few more words of advice and a few more wags of the finger, he turned towards Craven Street and was gone. I had mistaken the vicar for a 'Good Samaritan'. However, at least he had stopped and given some assistance, even if it had been for his own satisfaction.

The drunk gently lowered himself to the road and lay silently to enjoy the heat of the sun and sleep away the rest of the afternoon.

The 'phone rang, a dog had caught its feet in an escalator. I was on my way to the station, feeling relieved that my responsibility for the sleeping figure had passed. The drunk was asleep again and the vicar had partly fulfilled his mission in life by tending the fallen. The afternoon had passed satisfactorily. Tea would be ready on my return.

* * * * * * * * * * * * * *

There are times when one does not actually mistake the identity of someone, but misjudges the situation and later realises that one should have been warned about this misjudgement.

Like all professions, the veterinary profession has its code of conduct and the Royal College was there to uphold this. The subject of ethics, within the profession, was always under consideration and, from time to time, meetings were held to enable the speakers to give their opinions and the audience to air their own views.

One such meeting was organised in Dublin to be held at the Dublin Veterinary School in Ballsbridge. The speakers were the two Registrars from the English and Irish veterinary governing bodies and myself. I had been chosen, as I had recently obtained my legal qualification.

Ireland is not noted for its formality, and one has to expect a pleasant, though somewhat disorganised, gathering.

The meeting was in one of the lecture theatres with a long table at the front and looking towards banks of seats rising nearly to the roof. I had been to many meetings in Ireland and expected the audience to arrive sometime after pub closing time.

The two Registrars were less familiar with the casual nature of the Irish veterinary profession and started getting agitated when no-one had arrived by nine-thirty p.m., even though the meeting was supposed to commence at nine. I tried to calm their fears and warned them of the possible boisterous nature of the meeting, because the Irish, even more than the British, object to rules and regulations as to their conduct.

The first two vets strolled in at about nine-forty, each carrying two pints of beer. Others drifted in, mostly with reserve liquid supplements. We mingled with the audience and finally, in discussion with the organiser of the meeting, decided to start our respective talks. People still drifted in, until there were about forty, all male, practitioners.

Fortunately, I had spent many visits to Ireland and did not expect the audience to be particularly impressed with lectures on how the profession should be controlled by philosophical and ethical issues. Anyhow, they were already quite jolly and, on occasions, one or two members would drift out of the lecture hall, only to return with a tray of more beer. Heckling became contagious; banter was thrown across the room from one vet to another, obviously his rival in practice, about how he should behave in future and stop pinching his clients!

The three of us gave our respective talks and then sat back to answer questions from the floor. These ranged from fees, to advertising, to second opinions, all the expected day-to-day problems of the men at the sharp end of animal welfare and treatment.

Some of the questions related to quite unprofessional conduct and the two Registrars realised that they were only dealing with the tip of the iceberg in their routine administrative activities at home in their offices.

In the end, the organiser of the meeting [it was now well past midnight] asked for one last question before he closed the proceedings.

A gentleman stood up from the last but one row and asked for help and advice on how to deal with several cases that he had experienced recently.

This was what the Registrars had come for, to help their members in times of trouble and they leaned forward eagerly.

The first problem raised by the enquirer concerned a dog, which had come into his surgery for a distemper vaccination.

"At the time", said the Vet, " I was out of stock of vaccine, so I gave it an injection of distilled water, then gave the owner a certificate of vaccination and charged him for the vaccine".
The Registrars went pale.

"Unfortunately, the dog came in a few weeks later with distemper".

Part of the audience booed; they were obviously his neighbouring competitors.

"I told the owner that the dog had hard-pad" [distemper and hard-pad are in fact the same disease] and persuaded the owner that the two diseases were caused by different viruses. The Registrars passed notes to each other across me, as I was sitting in the middle.

"My second problem occurred last month. I had a horse come into my stables for tooth rasping and for vaccination. Unfortunately, there was an open tin of paint in the stable, which the horse took a fancy to. It licked it and 'went down' and, as it was in pain, I shot it".

The Vet looked round for more banter from his opposition, which he duly got.

"I told the owner that the animal had developed a twisted gut, and out of sympathy for the horse, I had to destroy it, as it was in so much pain".

It seemed that the owner was very grateful for this humanitarian attitude and paid up for the treatment.
The Registrars blanched even more and scribbled more notes to each other. Were they making a note of the speaker's name to 'strike him off'?

The speaker remained on his feet and continued in a rather pompous voice, which indicated that he was enjoying himself.

"Finally", he said, like a toreador making his final thrust, or a boxer about to deliver the 'knock-out' punch, "I had a recent case of a flock of sheep which I injected with a copper supplement, only to be telephoned several days later that a quarter of the flock had died. It turned out that I had already prescribed a copper food supplement and the sheep had died of copper poisoning.

I told the owner that, after a few post-mortems, I had diagnosed a magnesium deficiency problem in the flock and sold him some magnesium medication.

Could the gentlemen advise me, if I had done wrong and what I should have done?"

He sat down amid rapturous applause.

Registrars are not appointed for their lack of initiative and they quickly started to recover from their shock, but it was obvious that neither of them had a suitable answer available.

They looked at each other, and I realised what was in their notes. Between them, they had decided that I should answer the questions.

The Irish Registrar stood up and was met with a mixture of cheers and boos from the half inebriated audience.

"As this question related to pharmaceutical products," he said, "I think Mr. Ablett is in a better position than we are to answer it".

He sat down.

I might have been in difficulty if the practitioner had stopped after the first case of the dead dog, but he went too far with two similar cases of severe professional misconduct. Even if the Registrars were dumbfounded by these confessions, they showed no sign of relinquishing their serious and shocked countenances.

My knowledge of the Irish sense of humour was beginning to pay off and, within seconds, I thought that I had the definitive answer, which would not only let the Registrars off the hook, but would enable me to bring the meeting to a close with my own brand of humour and, I would have the audience on my side.

"My only advice to you, Sir", I said, feeling rather smug at the thought of my witty reply, "is to make friends with the

Chairman of your Disciplinary Committee".

I sat down feeling even more smug, but was to be outsmarted immediately.

"I am Chairman of the Disciplinary Committee", he announced. The audience cheered, the Registrars 'hot-footed' it to their hotels, and I joined one or two Irish practitioners that I knew.

All agreed that it had been a good night out.

SECOND OPINION
"I'm a second eleven sort of chap"
J.M. Barrie

CHAPTER VIII

SECOND OPINION

Second opinions are always associated with a vague sense of unease in one form or another. If one is treating an illness that is failing to respond to treatment, there is a feeling of inadequacy and perhaps a feeling of a possible misdiagnosis. There is also the fear that there is a better form of treatment available, which one is failing to give.

When a client approaches you and asks if you would object to that client requesting a second opinion, all of these fears come to mind, and there is the added unease that you should have already noticed that the client was dissatisfied.

Dissatisfaction may take an even more disastrous course.

I recall being in the surgery one day when Mr. Major announced that a client was waiting in the consultation room asking for an interview.

I walked in to see a middle-aged woman, neatly dressed and quite amenable in appearance.

After the usual, "Good Morning, how can I help?"

I was met with the request. "I have come to ask if I can have a second opinion on my dog".

This unnerved me somewhat, as I didn't recognise the woman as one of my clients. Maybe someone else had brought her pet in on a previous occasion.

"What is your name?" I asked.

"Mrs. Murphy".

The name didn't ring a bell.

"What kind of a dog is it?" I asked.

"It's a Bedlington Terrier".

That was no help, as I had not seen a Bedlington Terrier for ages.

I was getting nowhere, so tried a different approach in order to refresh my memory and before I got to the stage, where I might look completely inadequate.

"What is wrong with it?"

"It's his feet". That was a reasonable response, as Bedlington Terriers tend to have foot problems.

I was still floundering in a sea of incompetence so, reaching for the daybook, I had to ask the final question which would complete my inefficiency.

"When did I see him last?"

I hated to have to ask that question but had no alternative.

"Oh", she said, "you have never seen him. I have never been here before".

This reply gave me some confidence in that I had not misdiagnosed or mistreated the dog in question.

This confidence disappeared in a fraction of a second.

What kind of a Vet am I, if people ask for a second opinion, even before I have given a first opinion?

In a multiple practice, there is always the help of the fellow practitioner who, you know, will support you.

If this fails, then the time comes when it is necessary to offer the possibility of seeking the advice of an expert.

My expert had always been Professor McCunn. He was nearby at the Royal Veterinary College in Camden Town; he was always ready to help; he would never condemn you for the treatment that you had prescribed, but would praise you for what you have achieved. Also he liked the fees that he earned.

More often than not, you would use him not only for the difficult cases, but for the difficult clients, particularly if they were from the 'aristocratic' end of society.

I only used him infrequently and then mainly for Dachshunds with spinal problems. These long-backed breeds had a congenital problem with disc displacement and this was often associated with extreme pain, and no one likes to see an animal in pain. These conditions of Dachshunds were difficult to diagnose; there were no X-ray machines in practices in those days.

From experience, it was possible to forecast what the Professor would prescribe, and this gave me a chance to vaguely suggest what might help, prior to the visit to the College.

Perhaps a calcium injection might help, I would suggest, with a daily course of linseed oil. Anyhow, let's see what the Professor suggests.

We would meet the Professor in his office. His dark suit,

gold watch and chain and over-sized stomach would impress the client even before he shook hands.

His desk would be covered with books and papers and, in front of an ornate inkwell, stood a skeleton of a dog on a mahogany plinth. Whether there would be a skeleton of a cat, if his next patient was a cat, I do not know.

Having got the name of the dog, made a fuss of it and made a fuss of the owner, he got down to manipulating the poor animal's spine. Two or three trots up and down the office with the owner guiding it on a lead and then back onto the table.
The Professor explained the problem using his mounted skeleton of a dog.

"I don't know. What do you think, Ablett?"

He always treated me as if I was as expert as he was.

"I think a calcium injection might help", he continued.

This was his anticipated suggestion.

"Should we give it a try?"

To the owner he would say, "Calcium will help strengthen the spinal cord".

With that, he prepared a syringe with a 1cc. injection of a calcium suspension.

He asked the owner whether he or she would agree. If there was a positive reply, he would inject the suspension into the muscle of the hind leg.

With that, he would put the patient onto the floor and watch it run around the room. The owner looked delighted and generally remarked that it was ages since the dog had run around like that.

"Good", said the Professor. "I think a month's treatment on linseed oil would help loosen the joints".

"Can you arrange that, Ablett?"
The fee was paid, the Professor was satisfied, the client was grateful and I was exonerated.

But what of the poor dachshund?

He went home, having run around the room trying to work off the pain of the calcium injection, and was back to suffering spinal pain, together with the suffering of having to be dosed with linseed oil each day.

More often than not, the poor animal was 'put down' out of kindness.

In thinking back sixty years, one regrets not having had the availability of expert surgeons to correct these chronic problems, but veterinary surgery is now so much more sophisticated.

In the forties, it was necessary to notify the veterinary surgeon, who had been treating the animal, before one could start treating it as a second opinion.

This was not a common problem in the Craven Terrace practice. It only occurred in the equine side of the practice, if there was a conflict on an insurance claim.

Although Mr. Widden did get requests to give a second opinion in Pekingese problems.

* * * * * * * * * * * * *

The 'Old Man' had little time for bad horsemen, and although he did not expect veterinary knowledge from them, he expected a certain amount of common sense.

On the other hand, his main disdain was for other veterinary surgeons, who claimed to be experts, but knew very little about the heavy horse.

One such man was Scott-Hamilton, a well-known name in the profession, chiefly because he had written books on veterinary medicine, not only on large animals, but on small animals as well. I had never met him, but held him in some esteem because of his writings.

After several months in the practice, I was to meet him. A horse belonging to Charrington Warren, a coal company, had been hit by a lorry and had a damaged hip.

"It's got a knocked-up hip", announced the 'Old Man'.

As usual, the diagnosis was made in the stable just by turning the animal round.

"He'll never be any good. I'll send my report to the insurance company".

The horse was in the stables at Kew and had not been sent to the hospital in Kings Cross, as it needed no treatment.
Two or three weeks later, a call came through from the insurance company that their Veterinary Surgeon had examined the horse and found it sound. This would have infuriated me, but had no such effect on the 'Old Man', such was his confidence. "Balls", he said.

"Could you meet our expert at the stables at a date to be arranged, so that some conclusion could be reached". This request came via the insurance company.

In due course, a date was confirmed and the 'Old Man' was to meet Scott-Hamilton at the Kew stables at 6 p.m. one evening.

It was November and it had snowed fretfully all day but without the snow settling. It was cold and there was a bitter wind blowing.

The day before the meeting, the 'Old Man' had arranged for the horse to be harnessed to its normal cart with two tons of coal on it and to be ready at 6 p.m.

As usual, I had to drive through the wet streets down from Paddington to Kew. We arrived on time, but Scott Hamilton was already there standing outside of his car. After formal greetings, which were not very formal, as the 'Old Man' stayed in the car for the hand-shake, Scott-Hamilton stood back for the 'Old Man' to get out of his car.

The coal cart was loaded up with sacks of coal; the driver was sitting high up on his wooden seat, wrapped in a thick overcoat and with coal sacks wrapped round his legs and feet. The 'Old Man' shouted instructions to the driver to take the load round certain streets, in all about two miles in length.

This particular driver knew the 'Old Man' and had very great respect for him, to such an extent that he was already relishing a confrontation, where he knew who the winner would be.

"You'd better get up with the driver".

This was an order to Scott-Hamilton.

Did I imagine a smug smile on the driver's face? Perhaps it was merely the icy wind.

"Aren't you coming with us, Mr. Broad"?

Scott-Hamilton was showing the first sign of uncertainty.

"No", was the abrupt reply. "I know it's lame, you don't".

"Close the window", he did not relish the thought of getting any colder than he already was.

Car heaters were unknown in those days.

We sat in the car, trying to keep warm with a car rug, while Scott-Hamilton slowly climbed up on the raised driving seat beside the well-wrapped-up driver.

Scott-Hamilton had not come prepared for an exposed journey through the back streets of Kew, high up on a coal cart and in an approaching blizzard. He already looked half frozen.

Some 20 minutes later, the cart trundled back into the yard.

Scott-Hamilton was rigid with cold and dismounted with some difficulty.

He made his way slowly to the 'Old Man's side of the car. His joints were just about frozen up.

The 'Old Man' deigned to partly wind down the steamed-up window, just enough to see him more clearly, and looked out without saying a word.

"I can't find anything wrong with him", said Scott-Hamilton, half apologetically.

"Bloody fool", retorted the 'Old Man' and to me "Drive home".

Scott-Hamilton was still standing frozen to the ground, as I turned out of the yard and headed for hot tea and a fire.

BEAUTIFUL WOMEN

"A thing of beauty is a joy for ever"
Keats

CHAPTER IX

BEAUTIFUL WOMEN

There are few occasions in life when one meets a very beautiful woman. Perhaps the medical professions give one the opportunity to meet all types of people at a level, where it is possible to discuss various aspects of life, not normally topics of conversation. Doctors, by their very nature, have to keep a distance from their clients. Having seen so many men and women clothed, semi-clothed or unclothed, I am always surprised that they can have any liking for the human race at all! When I first went into business, my Director John Cochrane, gave me a piece of advice that has proved invaluable. He warned me that, during a business career, I would meet many people who could be objectionable and offensive.

"When this occurs", he said, "imagine them without any clothes on, and they will appear so ludicrous that you will not be able to take them seriously".

This has worked on many occasions.

Men and women, though women in particular, seem to be prepared to open their hearts to veterinary surgeons.

One of the most beautiful women, that I have met, arrived at the surgery one morning, elegantly and expensively dressed, with a large ugly looking Cocker Spaniel. Now, in the 1940's, Red Cocker Spaniels were notoriously surly and bad tempered, with dogs more bad tempered than bitches. Mrs. Cockburn, for that's who she turned out to be, introduced me to Rufus, who appeared to return my look of dislike and apprehension with one of defiance and warning. I have seen many veterinary surgeons approach a doubtful looking dog with the back of their hand, expecting to be bitten, and more often than not, they were. I had been bitten many times, and no way was I going to show any sign of fear in front of someone as beautiful as Mrs. Cockburn.

I grabbed Rufus before he realised what had happened and had him on the table in a flash. Mrs Cockburn looked relieved and Rufus looked shocked. Rufus had bad smelly ears, and this gave me the opportunity to suggest that the ears should be cleaned and that this would be best done in the surgery downstairs. It gave me the chance to get Jack, the kennel man, involved and Jack could handle most animals, mainly because he was adept at getting the dog's nose taped and its head in his unique kind of half nelson/head lock. The ears were in a very bad condition and needed an extensive clean up. Ears of dogs, such as spaniels, have a predisposition to getting infected; the warm moist conditions of the ear canals are ideal for bacteria to multiply and set up inflammation and ulceration. The smell becomes very offensive, and it surprised me that Rufus had been allowed to get into such a state when owned by someone like Mrs Cockburn.

I don't know how important smells are to the medical profession, but they play a very important part in veterinary medicine. One gets used to bad smells, but some are so nauseating that even veterinary surgeons find them difficult to tolerate.

The worst smell I ever encountered was in a young Scottie dog, which was brought into the surgery having continuous fits. The smell from its mouth was appalling, with a penetrating sweetness that permeated the surgery and lingered in the nose for several days afterwards. It was the smell of infected decaying bone. The poor animal was anaesthetised and the mouth examined. The whole of the upper palate had eroded away and, on examination, I pulled out a wad of rotten spiked grass seeds, the type that proliferate every autumn on grass verges. In fact, the whole of the upper part of the mouth was full of these grass seeds. The owner later confirmed that the dog was an avid grass eater. These seeds work their way forwards as their spikes only point in one direction, and they had penetrated the roof of the mouth and through the bone into the cranium, causing meningitis and fits. Treatment was never considered in this case and the dog was put to sleep.

One of these grass seeds may well have been the initial cause of Rufus's bad ears, as they so often are in spaniels and other floppy-eared breeds of dogs. Anyhow, the ears were dressed and cleaned and Rufus was taken back upstairs on a lead and wagged his tail furiously. He was so pleased to get away from the neck-hold that he looked decidedly cheerful. Mrs Cockburn interpreted this as a sign that he was feeling much better after treatment and that I was the man to treat

Rufus in future. Apparently, she had done the rounds of other practices and Rufus had had a field day with the 'back of the hand' approaches. Rufus kept his distance, but showed no sign of intimidation, which would have been counter-productive, as far as Mrs Cockburn was concerned. In those days, house visits were a normal part of routine veterinary business and, from then onwards, most of my attendances to Rufus were in Mrs. Cockburn's flat in Park Court, Paddington.

Mrs. Cockburn's beauty had been well recognised by others, as she was one of the country's leading models. Shortly after seeing her for the first time, I saw her photograph on the cover of Vogue, when Vogue was 'THE' only beauty magazine, devoted solely to fashion in all its aspects and had not been influenced by the modern competitive rat race of women's magazines.

Mrs. Cockburn had perfect facial features, beautiful hair and a wonderful figure; perhaps she was Jewish as so many beautiful women are. I coped with, and in due course, cured the ear problem, but Rufus was always needing attention for one cause or another. It seemed that there was no Mr. Cockburn around and he was never mentioned. The flat in Park Court was elegantly furnished, as you would expect from a top model, and was looked after by a daily help. She must have been paid well, because she continued to work there, even though she was terrified of Rufus . He, like all bullies, played on the weak, in this case, the 'daily help', but mainly when his mistress was away.

Shortly after I had been appointed Rufus's official 'Vet', I had a frantic call from the daily help, asking me to come over urgently – no other information was forthcoming and I expected the worst. The problem, which cost Mrs. Cockburn a calling-out fee, was simple, Rufus had got the 'daily' cornered in the lounge and wouldn't let her move. Fortunately for her, she was near the 'phone, but was already over an hour late in leaving for home. The door was on the latch and I let myself in and told Rufus to back off. He gave me a look, half of satisfaction, and half of derision, and settled down after an afternoon well spent.

Mrs. Cockburn was devoted to Rufus and perhaps he was the substitute for a missing child. Certainly, he was not the substitute for a missing husband, as I was to find out very quickly.

Veterinary practice in those days was simple and uncomplicated. One did what the client asked and did not get involved in unsolicited advice. If Mrs. Cockburn had asked for help in overcoming Rufus's bad temper, she would have been given a simple choice, either to have him put down or have him castrated. Those were the days before the canine and feline world was caught up in the peripheral activities of animal behaviourists, animal psychiatrists or dog trainers to assist troubled pet owners.

The Victorian anthropomorphic sentimentality had disappeared with the war, and humanity had reached base, where death had been only too commonplace and, subsequently, the loss of a pet was accepted as part of everyday living. Pets were to be companions and friends and served their purpose of what they had been acquired for. No one that I ever met was cruel to their pets and all were happy to seek professional advice, either from a private practitioner or from one of the charities.

Some weeks later, Mr. Major announced that Mrs. Cockburn was in the waiting room but without Rufus. She had come to me for advice as to whether she should get married again! The problem was not as to the suitability of the future husband, but if I thought Rufus would accept moving to a new home with a new cohabitant. The prospective husband was eminently suitable, he lived in 'millionaires row' in Hampstead in a very large house and, as I was to find out later, with two Rolls Royces in the drive. He had an impeccable war record and was putting himself forward for election to Parliament at the next poll, albeit in a constituency where he had little chance of winning. My advice was to go ahead and hope that Rufus would mellow with age. I heard no more for some weeks, but then read in one of the London evening papers, [there were three evening papers in those days; the News, the Star and the Standard], that Mrs. Cockburn, the famous model, had married Commander Abraham R.N. at the Marylebone Registry Office. The paper showed a photograph of the elegant couple.

Rufus was nowhere to be seen in the photograph, and I assumed that he probably had welcomed the future intruder into the household and had been persuaded that he was no real threat. It seemed that he had not been put into boarding kennels, as I am sure he would have been put into our kennels, if no other 'home' accommodation had been found. I couldn't imagine that he would have gone on the honeymoon with the newly-married couple.

Two to three weeks passed, and then at about ten o'clock one night the 'phone rang. There was no time for niceties; an irate Commander Abraham was giving orders to me in an agitated naval yell; "Get over here bloody quickly and put down this bloody dog".

In the background, the new Mrs. Abraham was shouting in an equally agitated voice, that I was not to come. Mrs. Abraham was my client and, to be fair to Rufus, I did not want to put him down, as there had developed a love-hate relationship between us over the years. I knew that, if I failed to turn up, Mr. Abraham would have no problem in finding another vet and Rufus's future would be in grave danger. So I packed my bag and headed with a great deal of apprehension towards 'millionaires row', knowing full well that the Commander could make mincemeat of me, whenever he wanted to. It was dark when I found the house; it was one of those roads where no house sports a number, which means that anyone, without prior knowledge of where they were heading, had to continually get out of the car and shine a torch looking for house names, whilst, at the same time, looking innocent to avoid the police being called for 'someone acting suspiciously'.

I found the house quite easily; it had every light blazing inside as well as lights in the garden giving it an extra air of importance. I parked my Morris Minor beside one of the Commander's Rolls-Royces and headed for the door. Before I got there, the door opened and what confronted me at first sight was a mock-up of Frankenstein.

A large figure stood before me as a silhouette; a figure dressed in a dark dressing gown with short Japanese-style sleeves, but what shocked me most was the horrible sight of both arms and hands completely swathed in bandages. It seemed that Rufus had been in fighting form. I was dragged upstairs into a very large and lavishly furnished bedroom to find Mrs. Abraham sitting up in bed with a very expensive pink satin nightdress, looking as beautiful as ever, but in a distraught sort of way with tears on her cheeks.

Rufus was sitting defiantly at the bottom of the bed. He gave me a quick glance of recognition, but kept most of his gaze on the Commander, following every move and uttering a low growl, whenever the 'enemy' came too close.

There was a high level of panic in the room, the Commander demanding in a loud voice that Rufus was to be taken away and destroyed without further ado, and the new bride shouting that I must not take him away and that he was to stay exactly where he was.

To add some sort of authority to the Commander's case, he started to unbandage his arms and there was no doubt that he had been badly mauled. I suggested tentatively that he should go to hospital just to get him out of the way, but was informed that the doctor was on his way armed with, I hoped, a tetanus injection and plenty of antiseptic dressings.

In due course amid the commotion, the Doctor arrived and took the Commander into another room to dress the wounds. This gave Mrs. Abraham and me the opportunity to have a conspiratorial discussion and we agreed that I was to spirit Rufus out of the house, board him for the night in the kennels and wait for her call in the morning. Rufus came quietly. I think he felt that he had gained quite a victory and that I was hardly likely to put him down.

I left without meeting the Commander ever again. The next day, a call came through that Rufus would be collected by the chauffeur and taken back home. I can only assume that without Rufus, the matrimonial harmony had been restored. I am sure Mrs. Abraham had been able to persuade the Commander to reprieve Rufus during the course of the night together, although the wounds must have been painful.

The decline in the heavy horse population in London, after the war was over, was dramatic and sudden, and shortly afterwards, I left the practice in Lancaster Gate and moved on.

Some considerable time later, my mother sent me a cutting from one of the daily papers, [my mother had a keen eye for interesting snippets]. The cutting was short and to the point. Commander Abraham had been found dead in a cheap flat in Naples with some suggestion that he may have been involved in gun running and that he had left all his money to his housekeeper.

The story had a final twist. It must have been three or four years after the Commander's death, that I got a letter from Mrs. Abraham. She had obtained my new address by contacting The Royal College of Veterinary Surgeons. Would I please telephone her at her flat in Chelsea, as Rufus was very ill. I was still in London, so I contacted her immediately and the next evening called at her latest home, a small but expensive flat over her milliner's shop. I was greeted with great relief, Rufus was lying under a chair looking very old and frail. Also in the flat was an elderly man, who was introduced to me as 'The Admiral'. Obviously, he was Mrs. Abraham's latest naval victory.

Rufus was dying and he seemed to know it. He couldn't raise his head, but did give me a faint wag of the tail in recognition. There was no discussion as to what should be done. A quick injection and that was the end. Rufus was to be buried at the Admiral's estate. We went round the corner for dinner.

Some days later, I received a Harrod's gift voucher, for twenty pounds, in the post.

* * * * * * * * * * * * * *

A woman does not have to be physically perfect to be beautiful.

However, Mrs. Abraham, for example, was a physically perfect woman; visually she was the epitome of what many European women would long to be.

Another beautiful woman was a frequent visitor to the surgery, but with a beauty of a different kind.

The main practice premises in Craven Terrace were in the Lancaster Gate area. In the mid-forties, this had a very mixed and diverse character. On the one side was the Paddington area, which extended to the Edgware Road. Small run-down flats in the roads off Sussex Gardens were inhabited by people of limited means, who were, on the whole, not animal owners. They were transient room-dwellers, who were trying to establish some sort of identity in a world, where identities had disappeared and had often been replaced by numbers. Ex-army men and boys had become accustomed to answering to numbers, women and girls to identity cards and numbered ration books. They were poorly dressed and of pallid complexion and saw themselves with no stable future; their worldly belongings stuffed into a suitcase ready to move at short notice, if a job became available or if their money had run out and the landlord was pushing for unpaid rent. What money came their way was spent in the numerous pubs around Paddington Station.

Praed Street at night resembled a pathway to some magnetic inferno with no escape route. These people, who lived close by, were the ultimate non-entities, never seen twice and never seemingly to have any end point; often people in transit from army to job or job to job. Their lodgings were interspersed by others, occupied by the numerous prostitutes, earning their living along the tree-lined Sussex Gardens. They emerged as soon as night began to fall and would accost any worker heading for home via Paddington Station. Many of them had pet dogs or cats and would call on us for treatment from time to time. However close they lived to the practice premises, they always asked for a house or flat visit and always paid up with cash.

To the south was Hyde Park with a better class of clientele, living in the South Kensington and Knightsbridge areas. Driving through the park was a five-minute journey. To the north and west were the poorer areas of North Paddington, Westbourne Grove and Gloucester Terrace; to the west was Bayswater just coming into its own as a higher-class hotel area.

The result of all this was that the whole spectrum of society trod the path to the surgery door, with each morning or afternoon surgery bringing its surprises.

Another beautiful woman, who was a frequent visitor to the surgery, lived in Craven Street, not far away. She had an insignificant white miniature poodle called Sky. Sky was middle-aged, about six years old, with slightly itchy ears, teeth that needed scaling every six months or so and the occasional flea problem. In the summer, Jack trimmed it regularly every month. It was a perky little dog, happy to wag its tail and always pulled the last few yards to get into the surgery.

Whereas Rufus was an aggressor, Sky was an appeaser. The owner was Mrs. Stewart who seemed, subconsciously, to realise that Sky was somewhat lacking in character and tried to compensate for this by adding external embellishments whenever possible. Sky had a collection of fancy collars, studded with mock diamonds and pearls, with varying colours of leather to match Mrs. Stewart's own outfits.

Mrs. Stewart was always immaculately dressed in what were obviously expensive clothes, even though clothes rationing was still operating. She was in her late forties or early fifties, which proves that beauty is ageless. She was small, but delicately built, with a clear pale complexion very well made up. Her hair was always perfectly coiffured in a light grey colour. She gave the impression that her hair was slightly powdered, as in the Regency period. She always wore the most delicate of perfumes and her hands were well manicured.

Jack got on well with her, and she rewarded this with a good tip every time he trimmed Sky.

One way of passing the time between operations, or while medicines were being made up, was to discuss the clients and their idiosyncrasies. With women like Mrs. Stewart, the conversation generally came round to the topic as to what they did for a living and what type of life style they had and who or what paid for it. Mrs. Stewart's background was a continuous source of discussion, particularly as she was so attractive and always so pleasant and cooperative in fitting in with trimming times and consultations.

Jack thought she was a very wealthy widow with time on her hands and no close family. Her income, which we all agreed must be quite large, was spent on clothes and expensive living.

No clues could be gleaned from her address, as she never asked for a home visit, and Craven Street had some very nice houses and flats.

The 'Old Man', however, who met her only in passing and then only very infrequently, saw her as a wealthy divorcee and that her ex-husband was probably either American or Italian.

Mr. Widden saw her as being separated from her husband, either on a temporary or permanent basis. Most probably, he was a diplomat, who came home when work permitted and that we would not know, if he was at home or not, altogether not such an unreasonable interpretation.

My own opinion was that she was a widow of long standing, who was still mourning her late husband. But this was a romantic idea, developed over years of inexperience.

Between visits, Mrs. Stewart was not a common topic of conversation; the war was still in everyone's mind and there were so many social changes occurring daily that no topic would last for very long.

Jack raised the subject out of the blue one morning with a startling announcement. Jack and his wife Jane would spend the odd evening in the 'Load of Hay' pub or at the Pictures. However, the previous evening had been spent in the West End and they walked back home along Praed Street at about ten o'clock and found themselves confronted with a fight in the middle of the Street. Now Praed Street, at turning-out time, was quite accustomed to drunken brawls, and Paddington Green Police Station was handily placed for dealing with them and, if necessary, St. Mary's Hospital was very close at hand to deal with the minor casualties that ensued.

This time however, there was a difference; the fight was between two women. Jack was keen to get a 'ring-side' view and managed to get a good look at what was going on, before the two contestants who, by this time, were rolling on the ground tearing at each other's hair, could be separated. Jane dragged Jack away, but not before he claimed that he would swear blind that one of the women was Mrs. Stewart.

He dropped this bombshell on us the next morning at coffee time, but as Jack was prone to exaggerate, not much credence was put on his tale. Anyhow, Mrs. Stewart was an upper class lady of some means; she was a wealthy widow; she was married to a diplomat who held a high position abroad or whatever image we had of her in our own loyal way. The matter was forgotten and of little consequence, as it turned out that Jane would not confirm Jack's story, claiming that he had had too much to drink at the time.

Would we have been so loyal to her, if she had not been so beautiful?

A couple of days later, Mr. Major announced that Mrs. Stewart was in the waiting room with Sky. I went up to see her with pleasant anticipation, as she was always very polite and cheerful and appreciative of everything we did for her. As usual, she was immaculately dressed in a pale-blue two-piece and flowery blouse; every hair in place; silk-stockinged legs and elegant shoes. Her make-up was as meticulous as ever, with a 'peaches and cream' complexion, but her meticulous make-up failed to conceal a beautiful black eye.

* * * * * * * * * * * * *

Women of all races, colours, nationalities or ethnic groups may be beautiful in our eyes.

London W.2., or more precisely, Lancaster Gate, in the 1940's was not part of the 'mixed culture' London of the late 50's and 60's. The influx of West Indian immigrants was only just beginning and one rarely saw a black face in the surgery. The earlier immigrant groups, mainly the Jews and Irish, were well established and integrated. It was uncommon to get foreign visitors with animals into the surgery, largely due to the rabies laws. Pets would only be allowed into the country, if the owners were prepared to pay for their quarantine for six months. Similar regulations in other countries deterred people from buying pets here and then wanting to return with them to their own country.

During a Saturday morning surgery one sunny day in July, the 'phone rang and a female voice with a foreign accent requested a visit to the Great Western Hotel at Paddington Station. The caller was a Miss Mansour and she had two spaniels to be looked at. Common sense suggests that visits to hotels are not the ideal way of getting involved in what may be an expensive course of treatment. It is so much easier to book out of a hotel without paying up than to sell a flat or transfer a lease.

A little gentle persuasion and Miss Mansour decided to get a taxi and drive the four hundred yards to the surgery. There was nobody else in the waiting room when she arrived, as surgery had closed about half an hour previously. Miss Mansour had two young black spaniels, which, from a casual examination, were in a pretty bad nutritional and medical condition.

A more detailed examination of the owner showed her to be rather ravishing.

The two dogs were skinny with runny eyes, but most noticeable was the fact that they had terrible skins. The hair or such that still remained was harsh and sticking up in all directions. Most of the coat had disappeared, leaving a black scaly skin with large scabby, inflamed and infected areas. It didn't take long to diagnose that both animals were suffering from follicular or demodectic mange, a most difficult condition to cure in the 1940's. This particular type of mange is caused by a small worm-like organism, that burrows itself under the skin and carries infecting bacteria with it.

It seemed that Miss Mansour was an extremely wealthy, unmarried Egyptian lady, who was on a world tour and had stopped off in London some three months previously and had bought the dog and bitch puppies to take back to Cairo for breeding. As she was heading for France at the time, she had taken them to another veterinary practice for boarding. She had returned that very morning to visit the dogs and had found them in a terrible state and had immediately taken them from the kennels back to her hotel. I gave her a very bad prognosis and felt in my heart that, in the end, both would have to be destroyed. She had named them Blackie and Lady and they were both very nice dogs, cheerful in spite of their condition and quite happy to give me a good licking when I picked them up. Miss Mansour was heading off to Paris, and there was no alternative but for me to take them in for treatment and boarding.

Miss Maria Mansour was a most beautiful Near Eastern young lady. She was about 22 or 23 with a flawless olive complexion. At least one always assumes the delicate slightly yellowish skin to be olive coloured, although to me olives are either dark green with a red blob in the middle or black. Nevertheless, her skin was of a perfect texture. Her hair was jet black and she had well-defined black eyebrows, dark flashing eyes and a rounded voluptuous figure, which seemed natural to her, but perhaps would be slightly plump to a European. She was dressed in Western clothes, but more highly coloured than one would expect in London, even on a sunny summer day. Not only was she beautiful, but she had the added attraction that she knew she was very beautiful and that always enhances a woman's attractiveness. She left the two patients with us, paid for two months board and headed for Rome.

Jack set about treating Lady and Blackie with twice weekly special baths, good grooming and good food. Their general condition improved and the coats took on a glossy sheen, but Blackie was a hopeless case, and when Miss Mansour returned two months later, we got her permission to put him to sleep. Lady, on the other hand, was responding well to treatment, the skin lesions were healing and new hair was beginning to grow on them. Lady didn't seem to miss Blackie very much, and being a long term patient, got special attention from Jack. And there were always new patients coming in for boarding or treatment and that kept 'old stagers' occupied.

Miss Mansour would keep in touch from her overseas jaunts by telephone and would return to see Lady at fairly frequent intervals. Early the following year, she was back in London, but instead of staying at the Great Western, she rented a flat in Notting Hill Gate and took Lady with her. That seemed to be the end of the case; she had paid up in full and Lady was cured. No doubt, she would be heading back for Cairo shortly.

One Sunday evening early in the New Year, the telephone rang and I answered it.

"Is that Mr. Ablett?" a husky voice with a slightly foreign accent enquired softly. The voice was immediately recognisable.

"Yes", I replied, "is that Miss Mansour? How can I help? Is Lady alright?"

Lady was fine, but Miss Mansour was ill.

"I am not well. I have a very bad headache. Could you please come round to the flat? I need some help".

Where Miss Mansour came from, you don't mince your words, you just make your demands obvious.

Now Lancaster Gate on a January Sunday evening with no surgery and no visiting was a pretty dull spot to be in. 'Your Hundred Best Tunes' and 'The Palm Court Orchestra' on the radio was about all there was to look forward to and, anyhow, who else could possibly be in London on such a day as to fire the imagination. The thought of a visit to Miss Mansour's flat stirred the hormones.

"Yes", I replied probably a little too quickly. "I'll be with you in about half an hour. Is there anything I can bring?"
That was a rather foolish question, for what was one to take to a beautiful Egyptian lady alone in a flat with a headache?

"Who was that on the phone?"

Although Mr. Widden was not on duty, he was in the sitting room when the 'phone rang.

"It was Miss Mansour", I said, "she wants me to go round to her flat straight away".

I was not going to disclose too much, unless I was forced to. My evasive reply was immediately picked up.
"What's the trouble?"

I had no alternative but to casually mention that she was not very well and that she had a bad headache. I elaborated on this to give my story some credibility.

"She sounded very distressed and she does not know anybody in London to help her. I think I should go over to see if she needs any shopping done".

My story was growing weaker by the minute.

"You mustn't go".

There was a firmness in his voice that made it difficult to argue with.

"I'll 'phone Dr. Brown and ask him to give her a ring and call on her, if she wants a visit".

What had started off as a dull Sunday evening in January and then moved towards an exciting evening with a rich Egyptian beauty drifted back to looking at the rain falling on wet streets and listening to the wireless.

My chance with Miss Mansour had disappeared for good, or so it seemed. No more was heard from her for several months, and it was assumed that she had returned to Cairo.

But, Miss Mansour was as persistent as I was disappointed.

The telephone rang one Saturday morning; it seemed that weekends were quiet days for Miss Mansour. She was once more back at the Great Western Hotel at Paddington Station. Could I come round to have tea with her that afternoon. This time Mr.Widden was not in the room and it was my afternoon off. "Yes", I accepted without hesitation and again probably too hastily.

I had the feeling that Lady was not the subject to be discussed.

I arrived in the foyer on time at three in the afternoon and she was as beautiful as ever. Wearing the usual bright colours and with her olive complexion, she was as enticing as she had been the first time I had met her.

She ordered tea and I started the conversation in a conventional way.

"Have you got Lady with you?"
"No, Mr Ablett. She is in Cairo".

"Is she alright? How's the coat?"

"Mr. Ablett", the repeated use of the name seemed to indicate to me some sort of intimacy. "Lady is very well and sends her love".

The use of the word 'love' increased the sense of intimacy.

"Stay calm", I said to myself trying to give the impression of a worldly professional young blood.

"How are you yourself Miss Mansour?"

I felt compelled to ask after her health remembering my last conversation with her, but at the same time not wanting to remind her too much that I had declined her request for help. The 'Miss Mansour' bit was added to enhance the intimacy. "Have you just come back from Cairo?"

The conversation was becoming very stilted, but I just could not bluntly ask what she wanted to see me about. I feared that it was merely a request for another supply of medicated shampoos and, if that was the case, I didn't want the meeting to end there and then.

However, I thought, if that was the case she would have asked me to bring a supply with me.

"Mr. Ablett", she said, "call me Maria", spoken with the same imagined or real sense of intimacy.

"I am going to Rome and then home to Cairo. Will you come with me? We will be back in London in about 6 weeks".

Miss Mansour was not one who dabbled with the cut and thrust of flirtation. She was rich, she was beautiful and she expected to get her own way.

I suddenly realised I was not the debonair young professional I had built myself up to be, but I was so overpowered that I just could not say 'No'.

"When are you leaving?"

This was an inane question, as I knew I could never accept such an offer, and there was no Mr. Widden to get me out of the hole I was in.

"It's very difficult", I stuttered, "getting time off at short notice". At least, I hoped it was short notice, as a delayed departure would give me less opportunity to extricate myself from such a formidable beauty as Miss Mansour.

I was frightened. How could I keep up with the obvious sexual demands of such a beautiful woman? I was mentally mixing up the images of the Kama Sutra with Egyptian belly dancers and was already feeling quite impotent.

"I am leaving next week", she said, "and I want you to come with me".

"Miss Mansour – 'er' – Maria", I started to explain, but she interrupted me with a delicate "Maria".

"Maria", I thanked God I got that out without a splutter, in fact it sounded quite professional.

"I have all my other clients to think of".

Five years of lying quickly and with conviction learned at 'The Ashby Infants School' in order to avoid Mr. Bramley's wrath was paying off at last.

Maria would admire me for putting my patients' health before the delights of her bed.

"I have a number of very sick dogs in the hospital at the moment, and their owners are relying on me for getting them well again".

Mr. Bramley had also been responsible for me to learn when not to overdo the lies.

I stopped there and began to feel like a man of the world again. In fact, I was already convincing myself that there were clients relying on my healing powers. I dismissed from my mind, firstly that Mr. Widden would soon put a stop to any such visit, and secondly, that I was scared.

I was playing this one at a very cool level.

"It would take me several weeks to be able to organise six weeks off from the practice. I would have to arrange for someone to take over my cases".

I hoped that Maria's knowledge of veterinary practice did not go so far as to understand that I was merely an assistant and that the boss could take over from me that same afternoon.
She got to her feet and the tea ended.

We said our 'Goodbyes'.
I left and slowly walked back to the practice, steeling myself to another evening of 'In Town Tonight' on the wireless.

Six weeks later, Miss Mansour [I mentally saw her as

Miss Mansour again and not 'Maria', as the intimacy had gone] arrived at the surgery with a young, six-foot suntanned German youth in tow.

He stood in the background in the waiting room, but even so, looked much more virile than I was.

"Mr. Ablett", she said and I thought I heard a faint hint of disappointment in her voice.

"I have brought this for you", handing over a long thin flaccid parcel. I took it and thanked her profusely and she left immediately.

I went up to my room and opened it to find a very colourful oriental patterned tie.

I never wore it.

Were there Freudian undertones in a flaccid floral tie?

The same question would arise later, when a beautiful dark-haired opera singer from North London gave me a pair of braces. This time, there had been no long-term treatment, but just two visits to vaccinate her poodle against distemper.

I never wore those either.

FRIENDS

"Animals are such agreeable
friends – they ask no
questions, they pass no criticisms"
George Eliot

CHAPTER X

FRIENDS

It is only in the depth of winter that one is able to know who one's friends really are. Acquaintances, gathered over the summer and autumn, leave, as the weather gets colder, and head for warmer climates and forget all about you, until the weather starts to warm up, and then they return, expecting to be met with immediate geniality.

But what is a friend? The dictionary will tell us that it is a person regarded with liking, affection and loyalty. The older one gets, the more doubt is thrown onto this definition. I recall a theological meeting one evening in Oxford, where a high dignitary of his particular religion spoke at length on 'Friendship'. After a long dissertation, he asked for members of the audience to give their definition of 'friendship'. Those trying to impress were very erudite, but a colleague from Indiana gave his definition as 'one who owes you money'. The speaker was not amused and was obviously not acquainted with the minutiae of 'Mid-West' philosophy.

This cynicism was not completely misjudged. I experienced an example of 'friendship' during the time I was 'seeing practice' as a student. It was in an expensive part of Middlesex. The Veterinary Surgeon had, by mistake, anaesthetised a kitten, opened it up, searched in vain for a uterus and, after a few minutes, lifted up its tail to find it was not a female, but a male. He sewed it up and quickly castrated it.

Evening surgery arrived and the owner came for her kitten.

The assistant was instructed to hand the kitten over and collect the fee. The standard fee was five shillings for a tom and one guinea for a queen.

"What shall I tell the owner"? asked the assistant, quite nervously.

"Tell them it was a hermaphrodite and charge them three guineas, as it was a difficult operation".

I was under the impression that this was not the first time this 'problem' had occurred.

The assistant headed for the door, but before she opened it, the Vet called her back.

"The owner is a friend of my wife", he said, "charge her five guineas".

This veterinary surgeon gave me an introduction into marketing. His waiting room was furnished with a thick-pile carpet and a mahogany corner cupboard housing several pieces of real jade.
"When my clients come in, they expect to be charged about five guineas, but leave them in this waiting room for ten minutes and they finish up quite happy to pay ten guineas".,
But I am digressing; the 'friends' I am referring to are wild animals.

* * * * * * * * * * * * * *

When the days got colder, I decided that those animals and birds which remained loyal deserved some recompense for their loyalty, so I bought a large bag of 'wild bird seed' and sprinkled some on the steps from the conservatory up to the garden at about three o'clock each afternoon.
On the third or fourth day, I was in the conservatory having a quiet doze and saw a movement around the seeds. I knew from the beginning that the local pigeons [or are they ring doves?] would be there, as they often sit on the telephone wire looking at me with heads cocked, so that at least one eye could focus on me, but they were not the first to overcome their apprehension for, very quickly, a blackbird appeared and began pecking the seeds and turning over the leaves. The blackbird is always around, so it was no surprise to see him there, although he seemed much more timid in the Spring and Summer.
Next to arrive was a robin; now, he only normally appears when the garden is being dug up, but he must have been watching from the hedge.
The arrival of blackbird and robin gave the pigeons enough courage to flutter down and bustle their way around the steps, as if they owned the place.

As I had expected, the next arrival was a squirrel. He appeared from nowhere and settled in for a good meal sitting on the fence, holding his takings from the steps and showing little sign of fear and was not in any way interfering with the birds.

Normally, when I move, the birds would look up, but seeing no immediate threat as there was a glass door between me and them, would settle down to carry on with their meal.

The squirrel, however, was not quite so genial. If I stood up, he was in the habit of looking straight at me and stamping his feet; he seemed rather bad-tempered.

That seemed to be the end of the visitors and I expected no more; the routine seemed to have been established. Some days later, a shadow moved up from the gap between the conservatory and the garden wall and, under the cover of hanging ivy, emerged onto the steps and quickly grabbed a piece of some flaky-like ingredient of the mixed bag of seeds and, like a ghost, glided back to its undercover escape. It was a rat. I had never seen a rat in the garden, although a visiting terrier had shown some interest in the space between conservatory and wall and I had assumed it was probably a hedgehog. My other visitors were unconcerned with his [or her] shadowy appearance and just carried on pecking and munching. It got dark and I lost track of them that night.

For several evenings, I sat and watched them appear in the same order to have their nightly meal – by the next morning all the food had gone.

I must say, that living alone, I had been presented with a new interest and enjoyed my 'friends' company for some time. Not everyone appreciated my pleasure and interest, as I was told many times, that I should get rid of the rat. If I encouraged my rat to stay, in due course, I would be overrun by rats.

"Get the Council in", I was told, or, "buy some rat poison".

How does one poison a friend?

So, I delayed doing anything, hoping the rat would go away, but he seemed to realize he was onto a good thing and appeared every evening for his dinner. All the visitors knew I was there, and we built up some kind of rapport. Yet, I was still being pressurised into getting rid of the rat, so much so, that I went to the local hardware shop and bought a drum of rat bait. By that time, the rat had become something special. The blackbird was 'The blackbird', the robin was 'The robin', the pigeons were 'The pigeons', the squirrel was 'The squirrel', but the rat was 'Ratty'.

Ratty was building up his confidence and would even spend some time eating his food on the steps rather than taking it into his hiding place. This courage increased to the extent that, one day, he walked up to the glass door, stood on his hind legs and looked into the room and straight at me. Was he just being friendly or was he looking to see whether he should join me in the house, if I inadvertently left the door open?

The pressure was still on me to use the rat poison and I succumbed.

The local shop had a good supply of rat poison, so I presumed it was a common problem in the village. I was still unhappy with my decision, as it seemed to me that the rat was the most timid and probably the friendliest visitor I had.

THE DAY OF EXECUTION

I had decided that I would add the rat poison to some bird seed and add some fried bacon fat to make it tasty, all in a little glass dish and hide it under a piece of wood to stop any other of the 'friends' eating it.

I read the instructions on the pack. **'The bait'**, it said, **'was particularly palatable to rats, which normally die within a week of eating the bait'.**

Just a minute!!

Was it going to take a week to kill Ratty? A week of possible agony or regression – surely this was cruel? Would the anti-cruelty charities condone this? Killing a fox by hounds in a few minutes was not acceptable and became a crime, yet steeple-chasing is still allowed. There seemed to be some double standards here because horses often have to be destroyed after falling at fences or walls. Even those rats, which were used in experiments, would be killed humanely, possibly by injection. Killing a stray cat or dog by poison, which could take a week to be effective, would not be moral and would probably leave me under the threat of prosecution. Why then is it permissible to kill a rat this way?

There appears to be an artificial animal hierarchy in human thought as to the place of animals in God's Creation, but this cannot be identified in the Old Testament.

Genesis has God creating 'living creatures of every kind' – there was no favouritism. Why should I pick on the rat? Why not the squirrel as well? He eats my bulbs and damages the thatch.

Rats are not vilified in the Bible; in some cases they even serve God's purpose.

In the First Book of Samuel, God used a plague of rats to terrorise the Philistines, and we thus see rats as God's agents. It is interesting to note that a plague of rats was not one of the ten plagues sent down by God to influence the Egyptians. It did seem, however, that some biblical writers were not quite sure in the use of rats to help God. The second book of Kings tells us that God struck down one hundred and eighty-five thousand of King Sennecherib's troops overnight and this was confirmed in the Second Book of Chronicles, but here it was an angel who 'cut off' the troops and this was recalled in Isaiah.

On the other hand, Herodotus, writing about the same event, described a plague of rats/mice invading Sennecherib's camp, and they devoured the soldiers' quivers, bows and even the handles of their shields, which left them at a bit of a disadvantage when going to war – they fled and many were killed.

In fact, the rat is not disadvantaged in biblical writings – it may take some precedence over his fellow vermin, the fox. The fox received the ultimate insult, when Jesus called Herod a 'fox'.

THE ECCLESIASTICAL COURTS

Keeping in mind that modern rat poisons were not available in the Middle Ages and that rat plagues had some sort of religious association, an ecclesiastical court in Autun, in what is now France, issued a summons against some rats, which had 'feloniously' eaten up and wantonly destroyed a barley crop. This occurred in the fifteenth century.

A defence lawyer was appointed, who succeeded in delaying the trial, the reason being that the rats were dispersed over a large area, and so a single summons was not sufficient. Therefore, he pleaded that separate summonses should be issued in all the parishes involved. Having stalled as long as possible, he then excused the absence of rats attending the court on the grounds that cats would be lying in wait for them on their journey to the court, and so their lives would be in jeopardy. This would enable a right to appeal. A positive result in the court would have involved the rats being excommunicated.

In the end, he won his case and the rats were excused. There seemed little chance of Ratty being excommunicated or anathematised and leaving in disgrace.

This recourse was not open to me, and I had little faith in the nineteenth century ploy of sending a message of advice to rats – by writing a note and stuffing it in their holes. These notes may be pleading, friendly or, in due course, threatening. One case is recorded where a note, covered in grease to make it more palatable, was stuffed down a rat hole, suggesting the rats moved next door, as the neighbour had a far better store of food in the cellar. The note was addressed to 'Messrs Rat and Co.' and ended with a warning that, if they failed to leave, the owner would be forced to use 'Rough on Rats', apparently some sort rat poison.

I felt it unfair to use this procedure, as the people next door are also very friendly.

In Scotland, messages were pinned to the walls of the house warning rats to go away or face dire consequences, if they didn't.

Neither history, nor the Bible, helped me to resolve my problem.

THE INTERCESSION OF SAINTS

But I had forgotten that I might succeed by getting some of the Saints to intercede for me.

St Francis would be a good helper.

Nicholas of Tolentino might help if Ratty got sick and, as his patronage includes animals, he might persuade Ratty to leave.

I would keep clear of Magnus of Fussen, whose patronage is against vermin, and I would certainly avoid Gertrude of Nivelles, who seemed quite definitely against rats.

Anyhow, maybe calling on the Saints might be worth a try.

THE END

The poison had been put away in the shed; Ratty still joined my other friends as one of those, who did not desert me in the dark days of winter.

I felt that, in the end, I must be firm and ask Ratty to ignore God's command [Genesis 1:22]. Please Ratty, be fruitful and multiply if you must, but don't stay in my garden and multiply.

PRAYERS UNANSWERED

Whoever I prayed to, ignored me; those Saints that I asked to intercede for me failed to change God's mind. His instructions were obeyed.

Ratty went forth and multiplied, for it was not long before I saw five or six rats suddenly appearing to eat the seeds. Ratty turned out to be a female.

What could I do? I put the poison down and, as declared on the label, after a few days, no seed was eaten and no more rats were seen. I hope they did not suffer too much, but I still miss Ratty.

In the veterinary world, one has to destroy animals, which may be sole companions to lonely people, but the trauma is lessened for both owner and vet by the fact that the sick animal may be suffering, so that destruction takes on a humane element.

Pain and death, and death particularly, is our outcome, but one has to learn to live with other people's distress and grief and try and alleviate it, whenever and wherever possible.

ASHES TO ASHES

"Earth to earth, ashes to ashes,
dust to dust"
Burial of the dead – First anthem

CHAPTER XI

ASHES TO ASHES

It was said that on the day war was declared, the exercise yard between the dispensary/examination room and the kennel area in the Lancaster Gate practice was piled high with dead bodies of dogs, with a few cat carcasses amongst them. It seemed that many people in Central London decided, on the spur of the moment, with the imminent invasion by the Germans and the expected bombing followed by the mass exodus to less vulnerable areas than London, that their pets would be better off out of the way. This attitude was more obvious in dog owners than cat owners, as cats were not so much kept as pets but as vermin controllers and, anyway, cats could fend for themselves.

This had no great emotional or financial effect on the practice as a whole, as it was in 1939, when, in a horse practice, dead dogs were not seen as a future loss in revenue. It was probably seen as a short-term profit-making exercise, as each destruction brought in either five shillings or half a crown, depending on whether the owner seemed able to afford the larger or smaller sum.

Regrettably, veterinary practice is not a perpetual series of amusing events. Frequently, even when the country is not at war, animals have to be 'put down' for one reason or another. The practitioner never enjoys this, as it is always associated with a feeling of sadness and some form of guilt by the owner.

Nevertheless, it has to be done and done in a humane way. Two aspects of destroying animals always have to be considered, pain and anxiety. Very often cats and dogs recognize a surgery either from previous visits or from strange smells, for the animal's nose is far more acute than ours.

In the forties, various methods were used to 'put down' animals, some of which would seem obnoxious to us now, but at the time were considered rapid, painless and not stressful; it also had to be cheap, for money was not a plentiful commodity.

In the mainly horse practice, the technique for destroying small animals was simple; the animal, be it a cat or a dog, was taken to the garage behind the boarding and hospital area, held firmly in a corner and killed with Prussic Acid. Here, the reader may well cringe and shudder at such a barbaric technique.

Whilst this was lethal to the animal, it held great dangers to the administrator. The Prussic Acid was bought in one-fluid-ounce blue fluted bottles from the supplier. One bottle could kill a number of animals depending on their size. The bottle was held in the right hand, with the right index finger over the opening, having removed the cork beforehand, and once the left hand had opened the mouth of the victim, a suitable amount of the Prussic Acid was tipped down the throat. At the same moment as tipping down the liquid, the vet or the kennel man would turn his head away, just in case the animal coughed and returned the Prussic acid into his face. Prussic acid is lethal, even if inhaled and would knock out anyone inhaling it.

Death was very quick, following rapid unconsciousness.

Prussic acid was used by the German hierarchy, when the Nazis were facing interrogation and trial at the end of the war.

Only once did I see a near catastrophe. The 'Old Man' was handed a medium-sized mongrel to destroy, just as he was about to leave on a visit to one of the stables. He was getting old and his reflexes were slowing down, the mongrel coughed and he got a whiff of the Prussic acid. He must have staggered back, as we heard the clatter and saw him sprawled on the floor. He was not completely unconscious and was able to make it to his feet unaided after a few seconds. He was able to confirm that he had felt no pain and that he had immediately lost consciousness. It proved to us that, despite any qualms as to the cruelty or otherwise of this method of destruction, there was no real pain or fear. Later, as the practice moved from dealing with equines to only small animals, the method of killing patients became more sophisticated and death was administered by injection.

In the twenty-first century, destruction is still rapid, generally without stress and pain, owing to the availability of concentrated barbiturate injections. Even so, during the war and post-war periods, other practices used different techniques; all were rapid, all were painless and most with little stress.

One of the practices that I attended, as a student, used an electric shock cabinet. The animal was put in the execution box, a collar put round its neck, and when the lid was closed, the animal was electrocuted. I was never convinced that there was not a stress element in this, even though it was painless; it was used in human executions in America, which gave it some validity.

Another practice used a pistol. The Veterinary Surgeon had a small .22 pistol and used some sort of dum-dum bullet. His technique, he claimed, satisfied all the requirements of ethical killing: painless, quick and stress-free. He used this technique for home destruction. He would ask if the owner wished to have the animal buried at home and, if so, would ask them to dig a grave for it. Then, he would take the animal into the garden, hold the animal near the grave and shoot it in the head. Death was immediate. Again, one may shudder at this method, but again, it only paralleled what was a known technique in human execution. Even so, it was not without its dangers. The Vet in question had shot his own toe off some two or three years previously, but this did not seem to worry him, and he was in the habit of relating this story to the client before the execution. I was never sure as to his motive for admitting that his aim was bad; it could have been to warn the owner what danger he was in and then charge a bigger fee, but this explanation is very flawed. More likely, it was to build up his macho image, as he always wore a 'Stetson' type of hat, and there seemed to be a cowboy image lurking in the back of his mind.

Nobody considered the British method of execution by hanging as applicable to animals, but one can recall that in medieval times, animals [very often pigs] were tried for any crime that they had committed, in the same way as humans; they were kept in prisons beside human convicts and, on one specific occasion, a pig was hanged in public for eating a consecrated wafer. Not only that, but the poor pig was dressed in human clothes and the recognized hangman undertook the grim deed. This Lex Talionis [the law of 'an eye for an eye'] reached its ultimate absurdity, when a pig that had badly mauled a child, was itself injured in its head and legs by the legal process of the time, so as to imitate the wounds that it had inflicted on a baby that it had savaged.

Death of convicted animals by burning or burying alive was more common, often associated with the same legal formalities that would apply to a human trial and conviction.

Captive-bolt pistols were used in large animal practices, and on the rare occasions, where a horse had to be destroyed in the street, the people who disposed of the carcass would be called out. I am happy to say I never had to destroy a horse in a public highway.

There was no real problem with the disposal of the dog and cat carcasses. They would be collected twice weekly and removed for cremation.

Most owners left it at that and were advised to buy another puppy or kitten straight away, unless the previous pet had died of, or been destroyed because of, an infectious disease. The very rare, rather neurotic owner would want his or her pet stuffed and mounted. In this case, he or she was given back the carcass with the address of a taxidermist. I only once saw the end result of this procedure and that was a moth-eaten looking body of a Dachshund, mounted on polished wood and standing on the mantle piece.

A slightly more frequent request was for the pet's ashes to be returned after the cremation – for the owners were always told that the animal would be cremated – so that the owner could scatter the ashes on the pet's favourite walk or in the owner's garden.

This caused no great problem because, when a request for ashes had been made, that particular animal was handed over to the driver in charge of collecting the carcasses. He was asked to make sure that he obtained the ashes from this specific animal and then return them the following week. For this, he got a packet of cigarettes. At a discreet time, after the animal had been destroyed, the owner would be contacted and informed that the ashes had been returned and were ready for collection.

Over the course of many years of experience, the kennel man, Jack, would know exactly what quantity of ashes would equate to the size of the dog or cat that had been cremated. Authenticity would be achieved, if the animal had been left with us with its collar and name tag, for they would have been carefully removed and placed in the old grate in the dispensary and set fire to with a handful of old straw and newspaper. The result would be a charred collection of studs, buckles and a name tag, which would be mixed with the appropriate quantity of ashes. The final cremation ritual would be for the ashes and bits of metal to be put in one of the 'Old Man's' cigar boxes [having soaked off the labels] and wrapped in white paper and sealed with sealing wax.

All of this may be considered dishonest and unethical, but the owner would be happy and that was our prime concern. Anyhow, he or she was never charged extra for the ashes or for the cigar box.

The owner was delighted with what he or she had received and would be contented that he or she still had some physical and emotional contact with his or her beloved pet.

Handing over the ashes was always given to Jack as, on most occasions, he was able to present the concerned sympathetic attitude of a fellow sufferer whilst, at the same time, extracting a tip from the grieving owner, who was at his or her most vulnerable.

Jack thrived on tips from owners, who had boarded their animals in the kennels or had them clipped or trimmed or cremated.

His major success in this field occurred one December day.

Lady Watson had, after many years of anguish, lost her Griffon. As far as our Vets were concerned, this was a landmark and nearly warranted a public holiday. Lady Watson had been a nuisance for many years, as her pet was partly paralysed, and her ladyship was forever asking for second opinions in order to get a possible cure. Sir Charles Watson was a gentle, slightly disinterested man, who must have got his knighthood for his work in the Civil Service, as I never remembered him making any decision. Her ladyship controlled the household, the dog and very nearly 'Messrs Broad and Widden'. Even so, we were sorry that the dog had to be put down, although it had suffered for many months with its spinal problem. Lady Watson had been a regular visitor to Professor McCunn, who would put on all the 'charm' for her [and doubled the fee].

As expected, 'Her Ladyship' wanted the ashes. As usual, they had been boxed in a special cigar box minus the labels; the box was from one of Mr Broad's best brand of cigars. The box was carefully wrapped in white paper and sealed with red sealing wax. For 'Her Ladyship', a special delivery was necessary, and Jack, seeing a profitable venture, volunteered to deliver the goods by hand. The address was only in George Street, the other side of the Edgware Road, so he set off on a bicycle late one afternoon; the wind was bitter and there was snow in the air.

Jack had put on a dark suit, the one he had been married in, with a dark tie and wore a bowler hat, a fair imitation of an undertaker, except that his bicycle was slightly out of character. This was of little consequence, as the address was a block of flats, and the cycle was left propped up against the railings for the porter to look after. By the time Jack had cycled along Praed Street and across the Edgware Road, he was white with cold and his nose and eyes were running profusely from the freezing wind.

The solemn act of handing over the box of ashes was, therefore, exaggerated by an ashen face and weeping eyes.
'Her Ladyship' was taken aback with this show of sympathy and reverence and, as Jack explained later, she demanded that Sir Charles hand over a large white five-pound note. He did this without a murmur and Jack left, probably still sniffing and wiping his eyes.

Before he had arrived back at the surgery, Lady Watson had already telephoned Mr. Widden to say how much she was touched by Jack's sympathy with a vague hint that it was a pity that the Vets hadn't shown the same sympathy during the deceased's lifetime.

This was one occasion, where we all agreed that she was

not advised to replace the dead member of the family with another puppy.

No doubt, we would have had Sir Charles' full support for this.

* * * * * * * * * * * * *

Death can be accidental or due to negligence. I can only recall one case where a dog died due to negligence, but the negligence was not related to a member of the practice, but to a third party.

A wirehaired Fox Terrier was taken into the boarding kennels for two weeks, whilst the owner was on holiday. It was a patient of the practice and had a daily dose of a branded tonic. The tonic was supplied by our usual supplier in large Winchester bottles for us to dispense in our own smaller bottles. The tonic was intended also for human consumption and was readily available in most Chemists' shops.

Within a few days, the dog suddenly became very ill, with convulsions, and died. We could not account for its death, even after a post-mortem examination.

We had no address for the owner and had to wait for her to call to collect the dog, when she returned from her holiday.

This was an unpleasant experience and Mr. Widden took on the responsibility of passing on the sad news. The owner, who happened to be one of the actresses in a radio 'soap', which was running at the time, was a rather objectionable woman at the best of times and acted the part of such a woman in the 'soap'. Even so, we could not object to her being very vitriolic in the circumstances.

At about the same time, I was attending a Pekingese belonging to a very rich lady, who lived in Grosvenor Square. She was very nice and often gave me food parcels to eke out the meagre rations that the Government allowed us. In comparison, the Lady's personal maid was always bad tempered a typical battleaxe. I received a call one morning from the maid to say the Peke was very ill. I rushed over to see a very sick dog having spasms. The dog was old, but not so old as to be having heart attacks, neither was it at an age, when it would be suffering from distemper. Anyhow, it had not shown any of the early symptoms of distemper. I was puzzled and prescribed a sedative and told the owner to stop dosing it with the tonic, which I had prescribed only two or three days previously. At that moment, my brain clicked – could it have been the tonic?

Back at the surgery, we all discussed the case and Mr. Widden noted that there had been one or two similar cases, but not severe enough to result in fits. In my mind, I had the inkling that the symptoms were those of strychnine poisoning. The tonic contained, as one of its ingredients, tincture of Nux Vomica. This had not caused any previous problems and the tonic had been used in the practice for years with no ill effects. Dogs are very susceptible to strychnine, but not in the small doses that we had prescribed.

Mr Widden called the Pharmaceutical Company, which supplied the tonic and informed them of our fears, and the next day their representative called to collect the Winchester bottle, which still had some of the tonic in it. But this was only after we had taken a sample for our own examination, if it became necessary.

In the meantime, the Peke had recovered, but the owner of the dead Fox Terrier was accusing us of killing the dog by giving it bad meat.

Two or three days later, we had a call from the Pharmaceutical Company to admit that one of their chemists had put liquid extract of Nux Vomica in that particular batch of tonic, instead of tincture of Nux Vomica [liquid extracts are much stronger than tinctures]. Mr Widden demanded a letter admitting their error and explained that the owner of the dead dog would be informed and that compensation would probably be requested.

The letter arrived and a copy was sent to the owner.
In spite of the admitted liability, the owner only demanded the magnificent sum of £5.00, when the company would have been happy with £50.00. The faulty batch of tonic was immediately withdrawn from the market – most of it was in Chemists' shops ready for human consumption.

In spite of all this, the owner still wrote to us saying that we had killed the dog by feeding it with bad meat!

* * * * * * * * * * * * * *

When pets are destroyed, either following the advice of the veterinary surgeon or at the request of the owner, there is inevitably a sense of remorse. Some owners subdue their grief by getting emotionally involved in another pet, others take the trauma more stoically, while others, particularly older people who live alone, grieve in the same way as if they had lost a human relative. Children get very upset, but a few kind words will help them on their way and, soon after the initial shock, are mentally stimulated by other events in their lives and particularly, if they are given another pet.

Adults and children are comforted by the belief that their animals will go to heaven, and they will see them again when they die. Parents often use this technique when a child loses his or her pet.

It is in these circumstances that the veterinary surgeon becomes vulnerable. He is expected to be able to give some authentic opinion as to whether animals have souls and therefore go to Heaven. This can be debated at length, but the converse is never necessary to come under examination. The converse being – do animals go to Hell? Most people consider that animals are not sinful. Even those, which appear to be cruel to other animals are only acting instinctively. The fox that kills all the hens in a hen coop, even when it has no need to kill more than one to satisfy its hunger, is not acting sinfully, but merely by some ingrained instinct.

If one looks to the Bible for help, then one finds oneself having to consider conflicting information. The following two extracts emphasize the problems of how to interpret biblical texts.

"For the fate of humans and the fate of animals is the same; as one dies, so does the other. They all have the same breath, and humans have no advantage over other animals, for all is vanity". [Ecclesiastes 3: 19]

"But ask the animals, and they will teach you; the birds of the air and they will tell you;

*the plants of the earth, and they will teach you;
and the fish of the sea will declare to you".*
[Job 12: 77,8]

There are those people who believe that all animals will have a soul and go to heaven, but these appear to be outnumbered by those who consider that only their animal has a soul – the cat owner, for example, will consider his or her cat has a soul but will tend not to give the same advantage to the cat next door, which continually and viciously attacks his or her angelic pet.

To us mere mortals, this will remain a mystery until we die.

Human euthanasia is not legal in this country, but animals may be destroyed without any restrictions, so long as it is done with the minimum of stress or pain. Pain is frequently the reason for destroying animals and relieving their anguish.

Defining pain in animals is difficult; the animal cannot tell you where the pain is and how serious it is and, it is in this context, that the veterinary surgeon has to use his own judgement. Experience helps, for all animals do not demonstrate pain in the same way. The horse sweats, the puppy yelps, the cat lies in an isolated corner. An overall clue is to look into an animal's eyes, and there you can see pain quite clearly.

The relief of pain is a major requirement of the veterinary surgeon and, in the nineteen forties, we did not have the drugs available to us that are now a common part of the vet's armoury.

We can use our own experience of personal pain to estimate the severity of pain in animals, but that is of very limited assistance.

Pain differs between species of animals and even between the breeds of the same species.

Heavy carthorses suffer cuts and bruises without any sign of great distress, where we humans would complain bitterly.

Dogs seem to differ in their response to pain, depending on the breed. Bull Terriers seem to have little sense of pain, whilst Yorkshire Terriers will demonstrate pain in no uncertain fashion. The larger the dog, the less is the response to pain.

I recall an Airdale Terrier that had been admitted into the surgery with a very bad mouth infection and terrible teeth; most of the teeth were extracted under a general anaesthetic of Chloroform and Ether, only to witness with astonishment, that the dog descended from the operating table and ate a bowlful of hard biscuits.

I have seen Pekingese with very ulcerated eyes showing little sign of distress, where we humans would be in agony.

Nevertheless, I have seen some animals with hairline fractures of leg bones screaming in agony, where other animals with compound fractures of limbs hop along, as if nothing had happened.

The age of the animal may be of importance in such cases, as hairline fractures occur generally in puppies.

Damage to cats' and dogs' tails, and particularly fractures [often due to them being caught in car doors], are generally associated with extreme pain. This may be due to the fact that the animal has no complete control over its tail, and it may be in continuous movement. Normally, an animal will 'rest' an injured limb, so as to avoid movement and pain, but it is unable, voluntarily, to control its tail movement.

The modern development of neurobiology gives the scientist the ability to measure pain by brain activity, but this cannot take into account the various aspects of species, breed, age and organ variations that are encountered in veterinary practice. Observation and experience gives the veterinary surgeon the ability to decide and act on what pain problem he is confronted with, on a day-to-day basis.

It depends on the veterinary surgeon's ability to analyse his patient's symptoms. The correct analysis will have its reward in developing the vet's reputation, and reputation is essential for any individual veterinary surgeon.

REPUTATIONS

"The purest treasure mortal times afford is spotless reputation"
Shakespeare

CHAPTER XII

REPUTATIONS

Reputations can be gained or lost, by diligence or accident, by good luck or bad luck. The 'Old Man' gained a reputation for treating heavy horses; the result was that he was a recognised expert, throughout the whole of London, in the treatment and diagnosis of equine problems. Some of his vast knowledge brushed off onto me and, with a master like that, my ability became more positive and grew as time went by. He got his reputation by hard work, diligence and many years of experience, but all these attributes depended on a sincere love of his patients. I spent many hours with him, as we drove round the stables of the various coal and brewery companies. I have seen him make a rapid diagnosis of the various lameness problems, which were so common in these massive animals. Lameness increased as the old wooden tarred blocks were ripped off the surfaces of the London streets and replaced by metal roads.

'Splints', 'bone spavins', 'bog spavins', 'pricks', 'laminitis', 'knocked-up hips', 'grease' and a variety of strains and sprains and other conditions of the leg were all part of the hazards that could affect the limbs of these animals. Some could be treated, others would make the horse unfit for work and thus became a financial burden on the company. The chronic cases would be killed and the owner could get some recompense for this loss by getting an appreciable financial return, as horsemeat was quite a valuable asset in the war and post-war eras, when food rationing was still very severe. I was able to watch the 'Old Man' make an accurate diagnosis of these various conditions merely by having the animal turned round in its stall. I never attained this level of diagnostic competence, and I would need to have the animal trotted up and down the mews, before I could come to some decision, as to what was causing the lameness.

Even though the 'Old Man's reputation was mainly in the London area, it must have travelled abroad because, on one occasion, he received a call from the manager of a 'Hungarian Stud Farm', asking for advice.

The manager had a Shetland pony, which he could not get into foal.

"Have you any advice as to what I could do?"

The 'Old Man' gave his usual abrupt reply. "Stop giving

it titbits", he said, "and get it to lose weight".

In typical fashion, he added his extra piece of help.

"Why have you got a Shetland Pony?" he asked, knowing full well the probable reason.

"It's for the children", the Hungarian replied.

"Get rid of it", the 'Old Man' retorted, "if the children ride the pony too often, they will finish up with bloody bow legs like bloody Buffalo Bill".

What the outcome was, we will never know.

Mr Widden, on the other hand, gained a country-wide reputation for whelping Pekingese bitches by using delicate fingers and forceps. His reputation was more widespread than that of the 'Old Man', as Pekingese breeders met each other in shows and exhibitions. The result was that breeders, mainly elderly women, would come from all over the country for his assistance, often booking the bitch into the kennels well before she would be ready for whelping. Caesarean operations were uncommon because of the risk of infection and the fear that the bitch would become sterile. Antibiotics had not yet been developed for commercial use, although the sulphonamides were beginning to revolutionise the treatment of bacterial infections. M.&B. 693, a drug made famous by Winston Churchill, was being prescribed in many common conditions.

The Pekingese was a very popular breed and good pedigree puppies would fetch high prices. The large head would always cause problems at birth, and Mr Widden saved many puppies' lives by gentle and skilful use of forceps. His reputation depended also on years of experience, patience and skill. It was not long after I joined the practice that Mr Widden was called upon by the Maharaja to fly to India, from where he returned with a most handsome reward.

A famous Siamese racing driver had been known to drive up to London from Cornwall, just so that Mr Widden could attend to his Pekingese bitch.

I am sure Mr Widden preferred small animal work to the horse work, and this may well have been due to the years he worked under the 'Old Man' without ever reaching his standard of skill. In the end, it was fortuitous that he did prefer the small animal side of the practice, as it grew as fast as the horse practice declined.

My reputation as a budding embryologist at the hands of Professor Amoroso was based on luck and my short-term knowledge of the eighth cranial nerve. The reputation lasted for half an hour in the exam room and then disappeared.

My reputation as a meat inspector never existed after the disaster at my exam.

But reputations can be lost by bad luck or a failure to concentrate. I partly lost mine one afternoon in Craven Terrace. Mr Major had answered the doorbell at the beginning of one afternoon surgery, came downstairs and told me that a rather severe looking woman was upstairs wanting to see a vet. He had put her in the consulting room rather than the waiting room, as she was the first client to arrive. I went upstairs and let myself into the room and was confronted, as Mr Major had duly warned me, by a stony stare and a responsive grunt to my "Good afternoon".

"I want to make an appointment for a vet to see my dog".

"Certainly ", I said. "Come into the surgery at any time".

I tried to be interested and volunteered what I thought was an interested question, in an attempt to melt some ice, at the same time hoping that I would not be the one to attend to her pet. I need not have worried.

"What breed of dog is it?"

"It's a Scottie", she responded in a very irate tone. "Don't you know a Scottie when you see one?"

It was only then that I spotted a timid dog hiding under the chair. Now, if I had been one of the modern dog psychologists, I would probably have diagnosed depression, due to 'owner-aggression'. But I was not a canine psychologist and just sympathised with the dog.

"If you don't recognise a dog like a Scottie", she growled, "I don't want you to see him. I want the senior man to attend to him".

So much for my reputation – how many friends she informed I don't know, but it was not the best of afternoons for me.

There are, of course, ways of retaliation and the most common way of revenge for a nasty cat owner's behaviour is to demand a urine sample in order to help make an accurate diagnosis. This request is not easy for the owner to deny, as urine samples are routinely requested in human investigations. It is virtually impossible in the case of cats.

Taking urine samples from dogs is slightly easier in the case of the male dog, but not quite so easy from bitches.

One dog owner was asked to collect a sample, not out of revenge, but out of necessity. I explained that, if possible, the owner should have a dish or a jar ready after keeping the dog inside for as long as possible.

In due course, the owner arrived at the surgery with a jam jar nearly full with a dark orange liquid. On close inspection, the contents appeared to be nearly solid at the base of the jar. All this seemed rather suspicious and I asked what she had done to get the sample.

"I did as you told me", she said, "as soon as I saw him cocking his leg, I grabbed the nearest jar I could find and got a sample".

"Was it a sterile jar?"

"No", she replied, "it was a marmalade jar, and unfortunately, there was still some marmalade in it".

People react in an abnormal way when under stress. Another client telephoned asking for help, and I was able to tell her to give the dog a digitalis tablet, which I had previously prescribed and supplied.

"Have I got any?" she asked.

"Yes, they are small white tablets that look like saccharin tablets".

"Oh! Fine, I have saccharin tablets, shall I give him one of those?"

Even more extraordinary was the client, who complained on a second visit to the surgery that the dog's suppurating ear was no better and the medicine that I had given her had put the dog off its food. In fact, the sulphonamide powder that I had prescribed was handed over with clear instructions to sprinkle in the ear night and morning, but it transpired that the owner had sprinkled it on the food!

Some events, however, were quite hilarious. I was treating a very fat terrier and was putting it on a slimming diet.

I suggested that, for the next three weeks, she should weigh the dog every week and write down the details.

"I've got bathroom scales, but I don't think I can get him to stay on them long enough to get a reading".

I explained that if she weighed herself first and then picked the dog up and weighed herself again, the difference of the two weights would give the weight of the dog.

"Do I have to take my clothes off when I weigh it?" she asked.

I should have learned my lesson of never volunteering or asking for information from my experience with the sour-faced Scottie owner.

Trying to help a veterinary colleague resulted in me being accused of causing the death of that colleague's cat.

I had left practice and was working for a pharmaceutical company and undertaking field trials on the newly discovered cortisone. At the same time, I was also working on nutritional products for newly weaned piglets.

On this particular occasion, I was visiting a veterinary surgeon on the outskirts of London to arrange trials at a pig farm. I parked the car outside the surgery, got my case and the food additive, and walked towards the surgery entrance. Sitting on a low brick wall at the front of the surgery, was a mangy-looking cat, half of its skin was bare and inflamed. At that time, cortisone was considered a cure for eczema in cats.

I greeted the Vet and, in passing, asked if the cat was his. It was his cat and I made the half-hearted remark that it was not a very good advertisement for his practice and, more seriously, suggested that he tried cortisone treatment.

Back in the lab, I sent him a supply of cortisone tablets.

Three or four weeks later, I called on the Vet again to check on the progress of the piglets.

"How's the cat?" I asked, expecting a show of gratitude for

the rapid cure.

"Those tablets you gave it, killed it", he said in a rather disgruntled manner.

This shook me, as I quickly tried to memorise what instructions I had written on the label. I couldn't understand how small doses of cortisone could possibly kill a reasonably healthy adult cat.

"What happened?"

"It got run over by a bus, and I'm sure that if it hadn't had those tablets, it would have been quick enough to get out of the way".

My reputation had gone with that practice.

* * * * * * * * * * * * *

Good luck, however, can earn a reputation.

In my student days, I had 'seen practice' in Cambridge. This Practice was run by a father and son, with an assistant, who was mainly responsible for the large animal side of the practice. The assistant, Bernard Over, was a large, jovial middle-aged man with a charming wife. Bernard was slightly deaf and this seemed to make him more jovial. He also liked his evening drink in the 'local', but he was not an alcoholic and maintained that, by socialising with the farming community, he was helping the practice's image.

Part of his responsibility was to attend cattle, sheep, pigs and those horses, which the owners of the practice thought below their dignity to attend. The son would attend those 'important' horses, mainly hunters and steeplechasers, which belonged to the bigger landowners. He always wore polished riding boots and that built up his image.

Bernard was called out, one tea-time, to attend a sick horse at a farm some seven or eight miles away. On arrival, he found a farm horse 'down' in its stable, sweating profusely. Horses sweat when in pain. He immediately diagnosed a 'twisted gut', which is not particularly uncommon in horses. The intestine gets twisted around itself, with the result that it becomes like a sausage that is twisted at one end; this cuts off the blood supple. In those days, the prognosis was very bad. If a horse remains recumbent for any length of time, it gets fluid in the lungs and death by asphyxiation and heart failure results.

Nowadays, expensive horses can be operated on to relieve the condition, but in the forties, this was not possible. Bernard gave the horse treatment to relieve the pain, but told the farmer that the case was hopeless and the animal should be put down.

Even so, the farmer said that he would stay with the animal, as he was fond of it and it had served him well.

"It is sure to die", said Bernard, but no matter how hard he tried to persuade the owner to have it killed, the owner persisted that he would stay up with it.

"How long will it live?" asked the farmer. "When do you think it will die?"

Bernard Over then did a quick calculation. He didn't want to be called out of the 'local' during drinking hours and didn't want to be awakened in the middle of the night.

"About midnight", he said, "ring me in the morning and give me a report".

He left and continued on his rounds.

Early the next morning, he got his call.

"You were spot on", announced the farmer, "the poor animal died exactly on the stroke of midnight. It was remarkable. How did you know?"

Spotting some form of kudos, Bernard muttered some comment on experience.

That seemed to be the end of it until the next night's visit to the pub.

Bernard was overwhelmed by his reception. Farmers were fully aware of his prognostic skills; he was offered a few pints and people at the bar wanted to be associated with such a skilful man.

His fame spread and, to the chagrin of the son, some of the son's pet clients began to ask specifically for Mr. Over to call and examine their horses.

How long this fame lasted I don't know, but I'm sure it continued even though, in the course of time, the reason for the fame would have been forgotten.

The son of the practice had a piece of history of which he

was very proud. On the mantelpiece in the waiting room was a Heinz salad cream bottle, in which was suspended a small foetus [about four inches high] with its head supported by a piece of thread tied to the lid and the hind legs weighed down by a small brass weight. A label on the bottle indicated that it was a foetus from a champion racehorse, which had been sired with a Derby winner. The mare had aborted and this exhibit, preserved in formalin, was the result. For some reason, this exhibit was 'the pride and joy' of the son, probably because it, in some way, associated him with a famous race horse

To his fury, the son walked in one afternoon to find a client holding the bottle, which now contained only a greyish sediment at the bottom.

"What on earth are you doing?" asked the son in amazement and anger.

"Well", said the client, "it says on the bottle – SHAKE WELL – so I did".

* * * * * * * * * * * * *

In the forties, advertising in any form was strictly forbidden by 'The Royal College'. Interviews to the media and public advertising was to be avoided at all costs. The practice of 'Broad and Widden', however, achieved fame, notoriety and an unenviable reputation one Saturday, by sheer luck. The kennels in Craven Terrace were used to house hospitalized animals, particularly post-operative patients, but were also used as boarding kennels.

One of the boarders was a Springer spaniel, owned by a rather wealthy couple, who lived in an expensive block of flats in Maida Vale.

The owners had gone on holiday for two weeks and had left their pet with us to be looked after. Whilst there, it was to be trimmed and shampooed. When they returned from holiday, they called for the dog, paid the bill and left quite happily.

The dog seemed pleased to see them, but slightly reluctant to leave. About three hours later, there was a knock on the front door of the practice. A stranger had noticed a dog sitting on the front door step barking to get in. It was the Springer spaniel from Maida Vale. A quick call to the owner was received with relief, as they said the dog had slipped its lead as soon as they got home, and they had been scouring the neighbourhood trying to locate it. They got into a taxi, thanked us profusely, made complementary remarks about the kennels and left.

Later that evening, there was a repeat performance with the dog again sitting on the front door step. Once more, the relieved owners were there to collect it, and they were told to keep it in for a few days. This time, the owner was most impressed with the desire of the dog to return to the kennels again, and it was difficult to restrain the admiration that was shown by them.

There the matter should have rested, except that the following week, we were presented by one of our clients with a copy of the local paper, enthusing about the love the dog had shown for its 'holiday' in our kennels, together with an elaborate explanation and a carefully drawn map as to the route that the dog had taken to get to us. This involved crossing the Kilburn High Road and other minor roads and then crossing Praed Street, both main roads with a reasonable amount of traffic.

It transpired that the spaniel owner had some connection with the press, and the press were always happy to get a story involving animals.

Our reputation spread quite rapidly, and I am sure it increased our takings, not only as boarding kennels, but as a caring and attentive practice. A number of clients referred to the article and congratulated us.

Dogs do get to like boarding kennels, as it gives them some contact with other animals and they never get bored, but this liking does not usually result in preferring it to 'home'.

We never revealed that, as it happened, the spaniel had been housed, quite inadvertently, next to a bitch in heat. It was only after the second visit by the dog that we looked at the bitch and discovered the real reason for our popularity.

FIRST AND LAST CASES

Epilogue

CHAPTER XIII

THE FIRST CASE

I travelled down from Nottingham to London on the Sunday and arrived at the practice in time for tea. I had been to the house several times before, when I 'saw practice' there as a student, so I knew which bedroom I would be having and knew Mr. and Mrs. Widden and their two-year old son.

The next morning, I started my career.

The first three days went very well, even though I knew that Mr Widden was going on holiday at the end of the week; the 'Old Man' would hold the fort. At about six o'clock on the Wednesday evening, the bombshell hit me. Those three days were spent just watching and getting a glimpse of how the practice was run.

"Ablett", the 'Old Man' said, "I'm going to take next week off, but I'll be at home. There's nothing special booked up, except for Thursday, when you will have to go over to Croydon and 'vet' a horse for purchase".

Part of the practice's contract with the coal firms was to 'vet' new horses for purchase. This particular animal was for the coal company, 'Rickett Cockerell'.

"This is just a routine check up for age, lameness and general health, prior to purchase. You just have to report back to them that it is O.K.. You can cope with that, can't you?"

"Yes, I would think so," I replied, feeling honoured that he had so much faith in me at such an early stage of my career. The feeling of euphoria lasted for about three seconds.

"There's only one problem", he said, "the dealer, who is selling it, is a bit of a rogue and he is also a vet. Keep an eye on him, as he will try and sell you a bad one. He's tried it on me several times, but I have no truck with him. Mind you, he knows his horses, so don't underestimate him. He won't know that I'm not coming, so you should be alright. If he starts moving the horses around as soon as he sees it isn't me, take care".

His voice had lost its air of confidence. In fact, it sounded quite feeble.

"Take care", he said again and my heart sank even further. What did he mean by 'take care', I thought.

The 'Old Man' thought for a minute and I hoped that, with a bit of luck, he would relent and decide to go himself, but I think that the thought of leaving his recent young bride and the fact that he was leaving the practice anyway, overcame whatever hesitation he may have had.

"The best thing you can do is to reject the first horse and have a good look at the second one".

All this seemed good advice at the time, but became less convincing advice, as the day approached.

The day arrived; the appointment was at two-thirty, and I decided to get there early and get a preview of the set-up to try and boost my morale. I didn't know Croydon, but used an 'A to Z' to get there.

Mr. Grasper, the dealer, had his stables in a mews on the outskirts of the town, much like any other mews which, in the next thirty years, would be converted to chic dwellings, much sought after by the 'yuppy' classes.

There were stables all along the mews, the street was cobbled, there was the smell of horses and the gutters were soiled with horse dung. This was not unique, as many of the other mews were still being used for their original purpose.

At two-thirty sharp, I drove down the mews hoping to identify where Mr Grasper, the dealer, would be hanging out.

The 'Old Man's description was very mild, compared with what confronted me a few seconds later.

From one of the stables emerged a tall slim figure of a grey-haired man dressed in riding boots and breeches of a dirty fawn colour and a red frock coat. To complete the bizarre picture, Mr. Grasper wore a black top hat. If I hadn't been so scared, I would have been amused. Picturing him without any clothes on did nothing to boost my morale, so Mr Cochrane's advice failed me on this rare occasion. But the riding breeches, boots and frock coat didn't complete the picture. In his right hand was a long riding whip. He looked like a third-rate Master of Ceremonies at a third-rate travelling circus. He cracked the whip a couple of times to warn me to move on. He hadn't yet realised that I was the 'Old Man's stand-in.

I got out of the car and tentatively walked towards him, holding out a hand in greeting. He ignored it and asked who I was. I told him I was from 'Broad and Widden' and had come to see the horse for 'Rickett Cockerell'.

I got a look of contempt, and he turned his back and walked into one of the stables. The whip was held firmly in his hand, and I had a sudden recollection that it was part of him, just as the cane was part of Mr. Bramley's anatomy, way back in my infant school days.

Three weeks before joining the practice, I decided to grow a moustache in order to make me look older and more experienced, but it suddenly seemed a handicap; my wispy, half-grown effort paled into insignificance when compared with Mr. Grasper's effort, which was twisted and waxed at each end and resembled that of Salvador Dali.

'Get me out of this, I prayed', but knew I had to sweat it out somehow.

Grasper was giving some orders to the stable-man, and I remembered the 'Old Man's warning that he might switch horses, as soon as he saw me. The stable-man led out what, to me, seemed a fine looking animal, a Shire, well groomed, the right size for hauling coal through the London streets.

I pulled the lips up and looked at the horse's teeth and, from my recent 'swatting up' of horses teeth the night before, it seemed the right age.

I lifted up each hoof and cleaned the odd bits of dung off with a hoof knife. One thing I was good at was lifting up horses' legs to examine their feet and I felt that this adeptness would impress Grasper. My confidence was gradually returning. The feet were very clean and in good condition.

So far so good, I had not made any major blunder.

"Would you trot him to the end of the mews and back", I asked the horseman. I decided not to say 'please', as I felt Grasper would not include 'please' in his vocabulary.

The horse was trotted up and back.

"Once again"!

This time, it was an order and I was vaguely beginning to enjoy it. Then I had it walk up and down a couple of times. All seemed fine to me. I then ran my hands up and down the limbs, hoping I could find some conformation deformity, but no luck.

Things were beginning to look black again; the horse seemed absolutely first class, and yet I had the warning from the 'Old Man' not to take the first horse shown to me. I felt sure that Grasper had changed the order, in which I was to see the horses.

I stood back and said with some confidence, "I don't like him".

This was supposed to be the 'master stroke' that would impress Grasper and let him know I was no 'push-over'.

Grasper, who had a complexion on the ruddy side to match his rig-out, went purple. He cracked his whip a couple of times quite close to me and let out a rasping, "why not?"

This floored me completely, as I had no idea why I should reject this particular animal.

"He's just not right", I said rather feebly.

"Why not," he repeated, his voice even harsher.

"He's just the right animal that 'Rickett Cockerell' wants".

"Not quite big enough", I replied.

Grasper muttered a few oaths under his breath, and then to the stable-man, "Get the next one out".

The next one looked O.K., and I went through the same procedures as before. Still, I could find no fault in it.

"This one's fine", I said, "if you would put it back in its stall, I will take down its description and let 'Rickett Cockerell' know".

I must get out slowly and confidently. I offered no hand to Grasper. He was still purple, but calming down a bit; the thought of his next scotch probably occupying his mind.

As I left the stables, I looked over my shoulder at the chosen animal to see it standing next to the first one that I had originally rejected. Suddenly, I saw that my horse was a good 'two hands' shorter than the one I had rejected.

The next Monday, the 'Old Man' arrived back at Craven Terrace. I had had no reason to call him out that week.

"How did you get on with Grasper", he asked.
"Oh, all right", I replied, "in fact, no problem at all".

As each day went by without a call from 'Rickett Cockerell', I felt easier.
It seemed that I had made a good buy.
I met Grasper several times after that, each time with some trepidation, but, as my confidence grew, the journey to Croydon became less stressful.
My moustache had developed and it wasn't long, before I felt mature enough to shave it off.

* * * * * * * * * * * * * *

THE LAST CASE
My first real case in general practice was vetting the carthorse for purchase on behalf of 'Reckitt Cockerell'. That case ended, more by good luck than good judgement, quite successfully.

The last case was one of pandemonium, trauma and a sense of inadequacy.

I had left practice some three or four years previously and was involved in research and development in a large well-known pharmaceutical company. The work, that I was involved in still related to animals, but in the area of producing vaccines and medicines, particularly antibiotics and steroids for the prevention and treatment of animal diseases.

I was living in North West London and had a call from a local practitioner one Thursday evening: I had known him for some time, but not at a social level. He asked if I could do a locum for him on the next Saturday. His usual locum had let him down and, as he was a motor-racing fanatic, he had arranged to spend the Saturday afternoon at 'Brands Hatch'.

If he did the morning surgery, could I do his calls and the evening surgery?

He said that he had booked only two calls and these were routine ones anyway.

I reluctantly agreed and the extra money would be useful.

It was all arranged. I would get a 'phone call after the morning surgery with the details of the two visits that I had to make.

The first was to a local house to give an injection of penicillin to an aging dog, whose owner was too old to visit the surgery.

The second was to make the monthly call to look at the guard dogs at the RAF station at Hendon. This was part of his contractual arrangement.

After that, I was to go to his surgery at 6 o'clock and stay until I had seen all the patients who came, and who were generally only few in number.

Surgery was to start dead on six and he asked me to leave the keys through the letterbox, when it was all over.

The first dog was duly visited and injected and I made my way to the RAF at Hendon. I was stopped by the guard, who directed me to the kennels; the handler was waiting for me and we walked past each kennel just for a check-up – no need to handle them – just sign that I had been there and leave.

There were about fifteen Alsatians; each gave me either a friendly bark or a warning snarl. One, however, had a small lump on its shoulder, which was inflamed and bleeding slightly. I had it brought out from the kennels and saw that the lump was a small tumour, which had been scratched until it bled. As a favour to the local Vet, I said that, if he brought it to the surgery at about a quarter to six, I would give it a local anaesthetic and remove the lump during a quiet spell in the surgery hour.

So far, so good!

I arrived at the surgery at half past five to see the handler with his dog, standing among six or seven other people with dogs on leads or cats in baskets.

This struck me as ominous, as I had been informed that Saturday evening surgeries were always quiet. Before I could open the front door, I was approached by one agitated man, who informed me that his dog had swallowed his wife's engagement ring and what could I do?

I took the dog in, gave it an emetic injection and said that I would keep the dog in to see what happened. Would he call back at about seven?

The surgery was, in fact, the front room of a semi-detached house and the waiting room was the hall, which was furnished with a variety of chairs. All that I could do was to tie the dog to the waste pipe of the hand basin in the surgery and cover the floor with newspaper and hope for the best.

Soon the dog was vomiting nicely all over the newspapers, but I had no time then to examine the results of the vomit.

I called the RAF handler in and got him to lift the dog onto the table. It was on a neck chain with a short leather lead and a muzzle. I quickly clipped the hair around the lump and injected a local anaesthetic all around the intended operation site, told the handler to take the dog round the block to let the anaesthetic take effect and come back in about half an hour.

He had a bit of a struggle, getting the dog out, as it had taken a fancy to the vomiting dog on the floor. In fact, every dog that came into the surgery was fascinated by my ailing vomiting dog, which was looking exceedingly seedy: I wondered if I had overdone the emetic.

Other cases were attended to without any problems and the dog handler returned.

There was now the quandary whether, if I continued seeing the other waiting clients and left the operation too long, the anaesthetic would have worn off.

I decided to do the surgery straight away and explained to the waiting clients that this was a bit of an emergency and they all accepted this.

The scalpel was sterile, the curved scissors were at hand

and the suture material was ready. Now was the time for some cavalier surgery, and I felt a bit like the old-time human surgeons, who, in pre-anaesthetic times, would get their fame by the speed of their surgical technique i.e. removing a leg in thirty seconds flat.

We got the dog onto the table; I got a swab of surgical spirit and started to sterilize the area around the lump but, at that stage of the proceedings, I sensed trouble; the handler had slackened his hold on the lead. Looking up, I was just in time to see the handler turn green and then white and watched him stagger and fall to the floor in a faint. In falling, he hit his head on the corner of the desk; he lay unconscious at my feet on the floor. I did manage to grab the lead with one hand and bent over the inert body of the handler.

Although I could handle unconscious animals with ease, unconscious airmen were out of my field. If nothing else, I thought it best to try and loosen his tie and collar and probably his belt, but that required two hands. I had to release he dog's lead, whilst at the same time, telling it to 'sit'.

I doubt if RAF guard dogs are trained to sit on command, but if so, this dog ignored my order.

I was worried about the dormant figure on the floor and started to loosen his tie. Although the dog ignored my order, it saw its master being mishandled on the floor and that, to it, meant trouble. With true canine loyalty, the dog leapt off the table onto my back with the result that there was a trio of bodies.

The handler was on the floor, I was bending over the handler and the dog on top of me.

Meanwhile, the vomiting dog had stopped vomiting and was perking up quite a bit with the interesting scenario taking place in front of it.

We wrestled a bit, and the handler started to come round, so much so, that I was able to leave him and started to wrestle with the dog, who still saw me as the 'enemy'. I was able to get some sort of control over the dog and was thankful that it was muzzled.

Soon, the handler was on his feet and I drew up the office

chair, so that he could still hold the lead whilst sitting down. The handler was still a bit shaky and still quite pale.

I told him to look away and set about removing the lump in double quick time; I put in two or three stitches and closed the wound, sprinkled some antibiotic powder on it and got the dog off the table. The handler was very embarrassed and carefully explained to me that it had not really been a fainting attack that he had had, but that the anaesthetic was rather strong and it was the anaesthetic that had made him pass out.

I did not add to his embarrassment by telling him that the smell was just surgical spirit.

In due course, I sat him back in the waiting room, telling him I wanted to see the dog in a few minutes, although it was really to stop him getting into his vehicle, being in no fit state to drive.

The other patients were attended to and all asked what had happened, having heard the commotion from the waiting room. Not only that, they all enquired about the sick dog that was getting over its vomiting attacks.

Although the clients were interested in the drama that they had heard, all the other dogs were very interested in the vomiting dog and wanted to have a sniff at the newspapers and their contents. One suspects that they would have liked to have 'sampled' the regurgitated meals.

Soon after that, all the clients had gone home, except the handler and the owner of the vomiting dog. I left them chatting together. I returned to the surgery and got down on my hands and knees, searching through numerous soggy pages of numerous daily papers, all of which were churned up and covered in a variety of the dog's previous two meals and saliva. Not a pleasant job, as there were no disposable gloves in those days.

But... success! I found the ring and returned it to the client, cleaned and unsoiled.

He left satisfied and the airman returned, with his patient, to the kennels. I cleared up, collected the day's takings, locked the front door, put the keys through the letterbox and returned home.

The next morning, the Veterinary Surgeon called to

thank me, gave me my fee of £5.00 and asked how it went.

I decided not to go into too great a detail, as I felt the handler would want his experience left untold. I did explain that I had had a hectic time and also explained that I had had to remove a tumour from one of the guard dog's shoulders.

"Oh that one", said the Vet, "he has had that tumour for months, but I was not going to risk getting bitten by taking it off. All I do normally is to give the handler some ointment to put on occasionally. I was not going to risk having to deal with a savage guard dog".

He now showed a little truculence!

"I suppose that means that I will have to take the stitches out next week".

I think that I earned my five pounds. It did, however, teach me that practice was too involved for me to want to go back to, although, if ever 'heavy horses; returned to the London streets once again, I would have a go.

THE END

ABOUT THE AUTHOR

Robert Ablett qualified as a Veterinary Surgeon in 1947. After some years as a student and later as an assistant, in a practice in Central London, where the main patients were 'heavy' carthorses, he moved to 'small animal' practices in Cambridge and suburban London.

Later he joined pharmaceutical companies and was involved in the research and development of medicines, antibiotics and vaccines for the treatment of animals.

During this time he was 'Called to the Bar' at Lincoln's Inn.

In due course he became Chairman of a large pharmaceutical company and later established his own veterinary business.

After nursing his sick wife for some years until her death, he matriculated at Oxford University and became, at that time and at the age of seventy-five, the oldest person to graduate there. He read Theology and, during his stay in Oxford, he was invited to the Divinity School at Harvard as a visiting Scholar.

After having graduated at Oxford, he obtained a degree of Master of Arts in Theology at the University of Wales, Lampeter and Master of Theology at the Pontifical University in Maynooth, Ireland.

He has recently published a book, 'Do Animals have Souls', a short history of the interpretation of Biblical Texts in Christian Theology, which has been widely acclaimed as a unique contribution to the place of animals in human society.

He is now completing his next book entitled "Charlemagne – the Christian Barbarian'.